Bizarre
COLORADO

By Kenneth Jessen

A LEGACY OF
UNUSUAL EVENTS & PEOPLE

By Kenneth Jessen

J. V. Publications
Loveland, Colorado

ISBN: 0-9611662-2-3

© 1994 by Kenneth Jessen

First Edition
2 3 4 5 6 7 8 9

Printed in the United States of America

Cataloging

Jessen, Kenneth Christian
    Bizarre Colorado

    Bibliography: p.
    Includes index.
    1. Colorado - History - Miscellanea. I. Title.

ISBN 0-9611662-2-3 (pbk.)

To my loving wife Sonje

ACKNOWLEDGMENTS

The original idea for a collection of bizarre and unusual stories came from my friend Lee Gregory. The result was *Eccentric Colorado*. Lee is author of *Colorado Scenic Guide* and was one of the editors for this book. The other editors for *Bizarre Colorado* were Bill Manci, Geraldine Hauber, Beth Nobles and Linda Oeters. This is the fifth book where Augie Mastrogiuseppe, at the Denver Public Library's Western History Department, has helped with photographs. Help on other photographs was provided by Rebecca Lintz at the Colorado Historical Society. The assistance of Philip Panum at the Western History Department was also helpful in locating reference material. Clark Secrest, *Colorado Heritage* editor, also provided valuable assistance.

Kenneth Jessen
Loveland, Colorado   1994

CONTENTS

INTRODUCTION

Bizarre Colorado is designed to be fun to read: the type of book one can pick up, read a story or two, then at a later date, pick it up again and read. Although some of the stories are quite serious in nature, humor is a primary ingredient.

During its early years, Colorado's economy was based primarily on the extraction of precious metals. The state also developed an agricultural industry. In time, the state's economy diversified into other industries including oil, transportation, and electronics. The key ingredient in Colorado's success was, and still is, its imaginative people. To develop the state's resources (both industrial and recreational) required experimentation resulting in both triumph and failure. Sometimes, however, the people involved attempted deeds beyond the norm. This activity, over more than a century, has produced a history both interesting and fertile for those seeking the bizarre and unusual.

The stories included in *Bizarre Colorado* show only one side of a given story. The reader is encouraged to refer to the Bibliography for more complete sources of information.

The material in *Bizarre Colorado* is derived from newspaper articles, books, and interviews. All of the sources are listed in the bibliography.

Kenneth Jessen, Loveland, Colorado

JULESBURG: A TOWN ON THE MOVE

Many Colorado towns have been relocated for one reason or another, but Julesburg has moved four times. Julesburg is in northeastern Colorado and the area was originally occupied by native Americans, including the Cheyenne, Sioux, Pawnee, and Arapaho. Following the military expedition of Col. Stephen Kearny in 1845, Congress passed a law to provide for the establishment of military posts along the Oregon Trail to protect settlers on their way west. The Oregon Trail crossed into Colorado's northeast corner. Traffic on the trail grew in importance after 1849 with the discovery of gold in California.

Sometime during the 1850s a French-Canadian trapper named Jules Beni started a trading post on the south side of the South Platte River. His idea was to capture business from the ever-increasing traffic along the Oregon Trail. After gold was discovered in Colorado in 1858, a new trail which headed southwest along the South Platte River, grew in importance. This trail branched off at Beni's trading post, placing the post in a strategic position.

In 1859, the Central Overland California & Pikes Peak Express, or Overland for short, was formed. Since the Overland's route passed by Beni's trading post, it was logical to make it a stop and to hire Jules as the station keeper. Because of its remote location, Beni basically could do what he wanted. A small town, known as Julesburg, grew around the trading post and consisted of a blacksmith shop, stable, saloon, pool hall, boarding house, warehouse, stage station, stables, and a few other buildings.

Trouble arose when travelers complained about the high prices Beni charged for meals and lodging. Beni also used the Overland's hay for his own stock. The Overland noticed some of its horses were missing which meant delays in its schedule. Thieves would run the stock off which, curiously enough, could be returned for a reward from Jules Beni. When the U.S. Mail began to disappear from Beni's stage stop, the Overland management became concerned. This could have resulted in the cancellation of the lucrative mail contract.

Joseph A. "Jack" Slade was hired by the Overland in 1858 to handle one of its divisions and to put an end to the horse stealing. Slade caught and killed some of the horse thieves, and his actions conformed with public sentiment. Because of their suspicions, the Overland Stage Company sent Jack Slade to Julesburg to find a replacement for Jules Beni. When Slade and Jules met, they seemed to have differences of opinion immediately and quarreled over trivial things. To further insult Beni, Ben Holliday, owner of the Overland, gave Julesburg a new name, "Overland City," but the name Julesburg stuck.

Beni brooded over Jack Slade, and the hatred between the two men nearly boiled over one day when Slade and a couple of riders arrived at Beni's ranch. Slade removed two horses belonging to his employer as Beni swore vengeance on Slade.

In the spring of 1860, Jules spotted Slade sitting on a wagon hub. Jules began firing at Slade with his six-shooter, hitting him with every shot. Not satisfied, Jules ran back into his house and returned with a shotgun. He emptied both barrels at Slade. As the smoke cleared, Jules said, "When he is dead, you can put him in one of those dry goods boxes and bury him."

To this, Slade remarked, "I shall live long enough to wear one of your ears on my watch guard."

Slade was carried into the stage station bleeding from

practically every pore, with thirteen assorted lead slugs in him. All of the witnesses of the surprise attack agreed that Slade's wounds were so serious that he could not survive. Beni was well satisfied that he had slain his rival.

The Overland coach arrived at this time and carried the road's superintendent. He found Slade writhing in agony and, upon hearing the story, had a scaffold erected for Beni's immediate extermination. Jules was drawn up by the neck three times by others more than eager to participate. Eventually, Beni's face was ashen from lack of blood. On letting him down for the last time, the superintendent extracted Beni's promise to leave the area permanently.

Slade hung on to life for several weeks and miraculously regained some of his strength. He went to St. Louis for further treatment. He returned to work as the station master of the Julesburg division, but he still carried eight of Beni's slugs. Because the attack was unprovoked, Slade was advised by his friends to kill Jules Beni at the next opportunity. Warnings were issued to that effect all along the Overland system. Slade elected not to hunt down Jules, but rather to let human nature take its course.

Jules Beni went about buying and selling cattle in other parts of Colorado. Soon after Slade returned to work, Jules broke his promise and returned to the Julesburg area to recover some of his cattle. At Cold Springs, Beni boasted that he was really after Slade to finish him off once and for all. Beni even displayed his pistol with which he proposed to do the job.

At Pacific Springs on the west end of his division, Slade first heard of Jules Beni's threats and of his return to the area. As insurance, Slade talked to the military officers at Fort Laramie (northeast of the present town of Laramie)

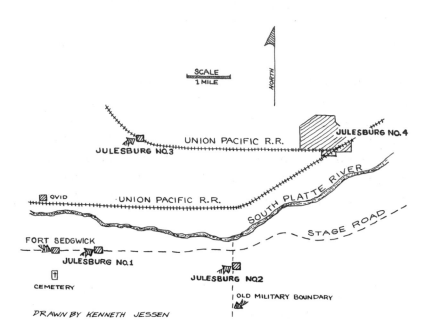

and followed their advice. The officers advised Slade to
seek out Beni and to kill him immediately. As long as Jules
Beni lived, there would be no peace on the Overland.

Next, Slade headed to the Cold Springs station with two
of his men. When Slade arrived, Jules was inside the
station. Beni spotted Slade sitting on the driver's box and
immediately ran out and around the building to find better
cover. He began shooting, but Slade's friends surrounded
Jules, forced him to surrender, and tied him to a post.

There are numerous accounts as to what happened next.
Some say Jules Beni was tortured by Slade throughout the
day, then killed. One eye witness claimed Slade hit Beni
repeatedly with the butt of his revolver until the man died.
Another account tells of how Jules wanted to make out a
will, and a passenger on the coach volunteered to draw it
up for him. Notes were taken, transported into the stage
station, and a will drafted. The completed will was taken to
Beni to read and approve. He accepted it, and the man
who wrote it returned to the stage station to get pen and
ink. A shot rang out, and by the time the man returned,
Jules Beni was slumped in his ropes, dead.

Others claim that the founder of Julesburg was dis-
patched by Jack Slade with two shots, the first hitting him in
the teeth without producing a fatal injury and the second
shot striking him squarely between the eyes.

Slade kept his oath in one barbaric act; he pulled his
knife from its scabbard and cut off Beni's ears. Numerous
eye-witness accounts confirm that a shriveled ear was used
later by Slade as a watch charm. To entertain the daughter
of an emigrant who stopped at a stage station, Slade put a
few pebbles in one of Beni's ears to make a rattle. The
little girl was content to play with this grisly toy. Jack Slade

jokingly used the ears as a medium of exchange. He would enter a saloon, order a drink, then offer to pay the bartender with an ear.

After the killing of Jules Beni, Jack Slade surrendered himself at Fort Laramie. As expected, they refused to take any action, and Jack Slade left the post as a free man. When the stage company investigated the matter, they showed their approval by continuing to employ Jack Slade.

Eventually, Jack Slade moved to Virginia City, Montana. One of his customs, when intoxicated, was to mount his horse and ride through Virginia City stopping at each saloon. He directed his horse into the saloon and, in the process, shot out the lamps and broke glasses. He also tossed the gold scales out into the street. The people of Virginia City soon grew tired of these deeds.

There was no law in the town, only a People's Court. A man with good character served as the judge. Slade stepped over the boundary of human tolerance after an especially violent drunken forage on every saloon in town. He defied the People's Court and threatened the judge with his derringer. The local Vigilante Committee voted to exterminate Slade. The committee arrested Slade, and one of its members announced simply, "The Committee has decided upon your execution."

The scaffold was nothing more than the gateway to a corral. Jack Slade was placed on a drygoods box and the noose tied around his neck. Slade was pushed from the box and died.

During the summer of 1864, the Indians attacked nearly all the stage stations and ranches along the South Platte River. The U.S. Army purchased a ranch belonging to Samuel Bancroft about a mile west of Julesburg and built a small post named Camp Rankin to protect wagon trains on the Oregon Trail and the South Platte Trail to Denver. Sod was cut from the virgin prairie and laid up in walls around the fort. Fodder for the animals was purchased, and thirty to forty soldiers moved into Camp Rankin.

Leaders of the Sioux and Arapaho joined forces with the Cheyenne in December of 1864 to put an end to the encroachment by the White Man. They decided to attack Julesburg, and approximately 1,200 Indians reached the general location the evening of January 6, 1865. Their plan was to draw the soldiers away from the fort, lure them into an area known as the sand hills, then ambush and kill them.

Early the following morning, a small band of Indians appeared near the fort. Riding hard, the soldiers came out in pursuit of the Indians. True to their plan, the Indians retreated into the sand hills with the soldiers in pursuit.

If not for a few over-anxious braves that charged out of hiding too early, the ambush would have worked perfectly. After heavy fighting, the soldiers made it back to the fort. In the process, half of the detachment of 38 soldiers were killed.

While this was taking place, the main body of Indians ransacked Julesburg. The residents had already fled to the fort. The Indians stole food and other items from the warehouse and cattle were also taken. The soldiers at Camp Rankin could see this taking place and opened fire. The range was too great to have much effect.

Several weeks passed and the Indians struck again, hitting the stations and ranches along a seventy-five mile stretch of the trail. There were not enough soldiers to be effective in stopping the raids.

As the captain of a detachment from Camp Rankin

paused on February 2 at the top of a rise about three
miles from Julesburg, he could see smoke in the distance.
Julesburg was burning and hundreds of Indians rode
around the town. The captain and his men rode toward the
Indians knowing they might face certain death. He was
hoping that the Indians would believe he was a scouting
party for a larger force. The captain used his small how-
itzer to show the Indians that he meant business. While the
Indians were preoccupied with looting and burning the
town, the soldiers managed to get back to the fort.

That night the Indians camped on the north side of the
river. They had taken many loads of supplies from the
store and warehouse in Julesburg across the frozen river to
their camp. Roaring fires could be seen from the fort as
the Indians butchered cattle and built bonfires with telegraph poles which they had pulled out of the ground. For
some reason, the Indians didn't attack the fort, but
Julesburg No. 1 was left in ashes. Noted Sioux Chief
Crazy Horse reportedly participated in the burning.

In March, 1865, Camp Rankin was reinforced and
enlarged. The name was changed to Fort Sedgwick, and the
number of soldiers was increased to 600.

For a time, civilians lived at Fort Sedgwick. A second
Julesburg was built three or four miles to the east of the
fort and just outside the fort's boundary. This allowed
liquor to be sold legally to the soldiers. It became a stage
station and a town plat was filed in 1866. The brave captain who led his men back to Camp Rankin became the
town's first mayor.

In June, 1867, the Union Pacific Railroad entered
Colorado and established a railhead just north of the river.
The residents of Julesburg No. 2 picked up and moved

to the railhead forming Julesburg No. 3.

The town was dubbed the "wickedest city in the west." A report published in the *Omaha Daily Herald*, July 10, 1867, told of how rapidly the town grew and how 150 houses were located in a four-block area. The report mentioned 120 saloons, several gambling halls and a few dens of vice. The population soared to around 3,000. The mayor, N.P. Cook, was a resident only five days when he took office, and none of the city council resided there over ten days. This Julesburg was violent and filled with many transients.

Out of its Omaha headquarters, the Union Pacific announced on July 26 that it was selling lots in Julesburg from $50 to $250 each, depending on location. It also announced that the town would be a distributing depot for points south to the Republican River and southwest along the South Platte River.

Violence in Julesburg No. 3 didn't last long. The Union Pacific moved its railhead west to Cheyenne in November. Since Julesburg was the nearest stop to Denver via the South Platte Trail, it continued to be a busy place. There was a constant flow of stages and supply wagons moving back and forth along the trail to and from Denver.

After the battle of Summit Springs a few miles southwest of Julesburg in 1869, the Indians no longer caused appreciable problems for settlers. As a result, Fort Sedgwick was declared surplus, and its doors were closed permanently.

In 1880, the Union Pacific began construction of a cutoff to Denver. It followed the South Platte River diagonally to LaSalle where it joined the U.P.'s main line from Cheyenne. The new branch left the U.P.'s main trans-

continental line a few miles east of Julesburg. The
Union Pacific named the northern end of its new cut-off
Denver Junction. After the line was completed the following year, it was clear to the residents of Julesburg No. 3 that
Denver Junction would become the principal town in the
region. They moved once again, took over Denver Junction
and renamed the place Julesburg. The town of Julesburg
has remained in this same location ever since, but there is
plenty of time to move again!

Drawing of Julesburg as it looked in 1865. (Denver Public Library, Western History Department, negative F9963)

INDIAN EATER

BIG PHIL

Big Phil, also known as Mountain Phil, was both gigantic and repulsive. He became one of Denver's favorite story tellers using his harsh voice and large hands to make gestures illustrating his stories. During a tale he would pause to stroke the ears of his huge dog. He was forever bumming drinks. When really liquored up, he told of devouring both of his Indian wives, an Indian guide, and a Frenchman. And if these stories didn't frighten a person, his dog did.

Big Phil's real name was Charles Gardner. He was sent to prison for a crime committed in 1844 in his home town of Philadelphia. He had killed a Catholic priest. Gardner escaped and headed west to the Rocky Mountains where he trapped and lived off the land. The Indians were impressed with his size and strength, and they considered him as being from another world. Much of the time, Big Phil lived with the Indians. During times when no white man was safe from native Americans, Big Phil traveled freely. For this reason, he periodically acted as a liaison officer for the government. One of his camps was located in an Arapahoe settlement at the future site of Denver along Cherry Creek. Big Phil was known all over the west, among mountain men and Indians alike, from Yellowstone to Arizona.

One winter, Big Phil and his Indian guide were sent by General Harney from Fort Craig, New Mexico, to Fort Laramie, Wyoming, with dispatches. A blizzard struck and, after trudging through deep, blowing snow, Big Phil and the Indian lost the trail. Their provisions gave out, but the two continued.

As Big Phil later recalled, "Ain't had a bite to eat as our grub gives out, and with snow a foot deep on the ground, cain't even see any game. I begins to feel holler in the flanks. So after livin' for 'bout five days on nothin' but wishes, I starts a-gittin' mad and watchin' the old Injun. I note him sizin' me up like I does him. I tasted man meat afore, so I figures to myself, 'Injun grub.' The next day about the time evenin' rolls around, and with my stomach rubbin' agin' my holler ribs, I can't get that Injun off my mind. So after we gits limpin' along for the day, I slips up behind him with my gun already cocked just as he's gittin' his roll from his hoss. Bang. He kicks for a minute or two. It's already dark and I hacks off one arm and fills up on raw meat as there ain't no wood for fire. I knows I cain't travel far without grub, so I hacks off the other arm and the two legs off at the hip bone, which I packs on the extra pony that I takes from the dead Injun, and starts out once agin' the next mornin'. They last me another week when I rolls into the fort."

Meanwhile at the fort, Big Phil and the Indian were weeks overdue. Then one day, Big Phil was spotted approaching the fort alone. He was asked what became of his Indian guide. Big Phil pulled a black and shriveled foot from his pack, then tossed the gruesome thing away and said, "There, damn ye, I needn't have to gnaw on you any-more."

Rocky Mountain News founder and editor William Byers asked about the taste of human flesh, and Big Phil answered that the head, hands, and feet, when thoroughly cooked, tasted good, not unlike pork. But the other por-tions of the body did not suit the cannibal because they were too gristly and tough.

Kit Carson and his companions came through what was to become the city of Denver and found Big Phil living in a tepee with his squaw, Kloock. Kit Carson asked Big Phil to

trap for him, but said that none of his men wanted to stay with him (or for that matter, walk ahead of him on a trail). The following spring, one of Carson's men, Charlie Jones, stopped by to see if Big Phil needed supplies. Upon his return to Kit Carson's camp, Jones reported, "It seems Mountain Phil has been faring better than any of us, for he had been able to kill his meat at camp, thereby saving him the trouble of having to get out and hunt for it." Jones continued, "Boys, if I should tell you what I know about Mountain Phil, you never would believe it, but as sure as you live, he had killed his squaw and eaten most of her."

It is generally believed that Big Phil was killed in Montana around 1874.

KEN JESSEN

WILLIAM S. WILLIAMS, M.T.

Mountain men like William Sherley "Old Bill" Williams were a breed apart. They lived the life of free trappers and pathfinders. They had their own way of expressing themselves and led a solitary way of life. William S. Williams insisted that his name be followed by the letters "M.T." He felt he had earned his degree as Master Trapper.

At one time, Old Bill became involved in a quarrel with a Blackfoot Indian. They decided to fight to the death in true Indian tradition. Williams soon had the Indian down and grabbed his scalp-lock. The Indian shouted, "Bill Williams!" and pleaded for his life.

The response from the mountain man demanded respect, "William S. Williams. M.T., if you please." He then used his knife to remove the Indian's scalp.

William S. Williams lived more than half of his life in the mountains. He told people that he was never anywhere else, and claimed he rolled out of a thunderstorm in the mountains and remembered nothing else. At other times, Williams told people he was "translated" from the Great Bear constellation for some special purpose to be made known to him in the hereafter. Actually, he was once a Methodist minister and had a good education.

There is one particular story that reveals the nature of William S. Williams, M.T. It involves a young man who accidentally wandered into his camp.

"Hum!" remarked Williams, "Here comes another enormous fool of a young rascal to crowd us here in the mountains. We shan't have an inch of elbow room left!"

As he was turning over a lump of dough on the coals of his fire with his toes (which protruded through his moccasins) he said, "Cook old cake. Here comes a white fool, and he's hungry of course." Looking at the young visitor,

Williams said, " Now, you miserable young blockhead, do you know me?"

The boy said, "I guess I do."

"You guess," replied Williams, "You're a pretty sample of a scalp-lock to come here guessing. Had you nobody to keep you at home that you must come strolling out here among the bears and Blackfeet? How do you know me?"

The only answer the boy could muster was, "I reckon I guess."

"Oh, you're a big figure at mathematics! You had better get rid of your guessing and your reckoning if you want to live among the rocks. Take up that chunk of burnt dough there, and stuff it down your ravenous maw!"

"Thank you - I'm not hungry," replied the boy.

The old trapper continued his lecture, "Don't come here to tell lies, sir. We are honest men in the mountains and you mustn't come here to contaminate us with your civilization. You are hungry, and you know it, and you must eat that cake. I've got another. Do you take me for an antediluvian, not to share my dinner with you?"

As the boy devoured the cake he asked, "Ain't you the man they call Bill Williams?"

Bill roared back, "What do they call me?"

"William Williams, I think!" was the rather timid answer from the boy in a tone of respect toward his benefactor.

"William S. Williams, M.T., you young buzzard's meat!" replied the old trapper. He continued, "Look here, boy, do you see that butte? There's a hole in it, and there's where I put my bones."

"Bones!" exclaimed the bewildered young man.

"Yes - wah!" continued Bill as he lifted his rifle as though to shoot, "There's where I bury my dead; that's my

bone-house."

"Why you don't..." began the lad.

"Don't tell me I don't," interrupted the old trapper, "or I'll 'don't you', knock me dead if I don't. How would (you) like to sleep there tonight? Eat away and don't be gaping at a natural Christian like a born fool. I always stow away my white bones decently. Eat away you stupid young block-head, and stop staring. I dare say you call yourself a gentle-man!"

"Ye-es!" said the boy now realizing he had encountered one of Colorado's most eccentric residents.

Having thoroughly intimidated the boy, Bill now intro-duced himself, "Happy of your acquaintance. If you have done eating, just remember that you have dined with Wil-liam S. Williams, M.T."

THE DEADLY
RAT GAME

Because "Uncle" Billy Cozens was a young man with a craving for adventure, he set out from his home in New York State around 1859 and headed for Colorado to prospect for gold. He reached Black Hawk nearly out of money.

Jack Kehler operated a store which was located in a long, low cabin in Black Hawk. It, like everything else in town, showed signs of having been built in a great hurry. No chinking was used between the logs. This made the structure cold and drafty. In the corner of the store, Jack had set up a bar on rough planks spanning a couple of barrels. Assorted bottles of gin, brandy, and whiskey were haphazardly placed on three plank shelves on the cabin wall behind the makeshift bar. Smoking tobacco and a few plugs of chewing tobacco were also kept on the shelves. A little tin cup on the bottom shelf held the gold dust Jack took in trade for drinks. The price for a drink was as much gold dust as the bartender could remove from the miner's pouch with two fingers in one pinch.

At the back of the store and across from the bar was a big pile of flour sacks. Jack spread blankets on top of the pile and slept there during the night.

The rest of the store was filled with boxes and barrels containing supplies. When a new shipment arrived, Jack would unload the merchandise into the nearest empty space. He would pry open a box of goods and sell the merchandise directly from the box without moving it until it was empty.

Young Cozens entered and looked around Jack Kehler's store-combination-bar and decided to use some of his money to buy a drink. When he paid Jack in currency, Kehler remarked, "Hub, tenderfoot money! Must be a new arrival! When'd ye get in?"

"Yes," replied Cozens, "Damn new and damn near broke, and I am looking for a job."

When Kehler found out that Cozens had worked as a carpenter, he asked, "Think you could chink up this building and make a tight job of it, young feller?"

Cozens guaranteed that if he didn't do a good job of chinking the walls Kehler would not owe him a cent. In three days the log building was nicely chinked and tight. After being paid a liberal sum, Jack asked, "Ever tend bar, Billy?"

After finding that Cozens knew absolutely nothing about tending bar, Jack said, "Th'aint much to it to learn. All you got to do is to keep sober when the other boys is fillin' up and jest give'em all they want to buy so long as their dust lasts to pay for it, and don't let any whiskey go out on tick <sic>. The hours is purty long for me, and I'm needin' a clerk...some young feller who can tend bar and sell the groceries. If you want the job, Billy, you can have it." With this, Billy Cozens went to work tending bar and selling groceries.

The store had a dirt floor, and rats dug tunnels under the lowest layer of logs to get inside. They also raced around the walls inside the chinking. The rats were quite numerous, and Jack, using his expert shooting ability, picked them off as he sat on the pile of flour sacks.

One day, just as Billy finished his day's work, a big, fat rat ran along the top of the wall behind his head. Without warning, Jack blew the rat to kingdom come, and the blood spattered all over Billy. The fact that Billy jumped off the ground just amused Jack. He laughed and said, "Nuthin' to get nervous about, Billy, I was jest killin' a rat!" He then

"Uncle" Billy Cozens as a young man. After his early experiences in Black Hawk, he later became sheriff of Gilpin County and lived many years in Central City. (Denver Public Library, Western History Department, negative F27016)

laid back on the flour sacks and laughed.

Several days passed, and Jack once again used his revolver to suddenly blast another rat from behind the bar where Billy was serving. Billy again jumped, and Jack said, "No need to jump, Billy! I was jest killin' a rat!"

A week went by without any rats getting behind the bar. One day, Billy set a gin bottle back on the shelf and Jack shot another rat. The rat, however, was on the same shelf, and the bullet broke the bottle between Billy's fingers. Billy not only jumped but yelled at Jack. Again Jack only laughed and said, "Nuthin' to be bothered about! I had to kill the rat!"

Billy was also familiar with the use of firearms and had enough of Jack's deadly rat game. One afternoon, Jack dozed off on his flour-sack bed. Billy spotted a big, fat rat running along the upper log. He waited until the rat was right over Jack's head. Billy took aim and fired. The bullet was a little low and clipped a piece out of Jack's ear. He woke up instantly and reached for the remainder of his ear. He first looked at his blood-covered hand, then back at Billy holding the smoking revolver.

Quick of wit, Billy retorted, "Oh nuthin' to get nervous about, Jack! I was only killin' a rat!"

Jack again grabbed his ear then looked at the fresh blood on his hand. He said sternly, "Billy! You and me ain't goin' to play that rat game anymore!"

Jack Kehler became sheriff of what was then Arapahoe County, and Billy Cozens became his chief deputy. When Gilpin County was formed from Arapahoe County, Billy took over the job as sheriff.

THE PICKLED
SKULL MYSTERY

A half-dozen Texas Rangers got wind of a rich gold strike in South Park during 1863. This prompted the Rangers to ride north to check things over. Their destination was the new Colorado mining camp of Montgomery, located at the foot of Hoosier Pass and at the headwaters of the South Platte River. Montgomery had already hit its peak by this time and had became the largest community in the entire South Park region.

One evening, the Rangers decided to explore the foothills. During their ride, they spotted an encampment of Ute Indians belonging to Chief Colorow. Low on rations, the Texans boldly rode into the Indian camp. Colorow had mixed feeling about white men, but decided to help the Rangers by giving them some fresh meat and assigning them a place to camp.

The Rangers took note of the Indian ponies. During a dinner of fresh antelope steaks provided by the Indians, the Rangers discussed the question of stealing some of the ponies.

At dawn, Colorow's braves got ready to organize a hunting party. Boys were sent to find the swiftest mounts from the herd, and quickly discovered that a dozen of their best ponies were missing. Their Texan guests were also gone, and the ashes of their camp fire were nearly cold.

The hunting party quickly switched to war paint and took after the Texas horse thieves. The trail led past Fairplay and into heavy timber. The Rangers knew the Indians would follow and took a circuitous route back toward Montgomery. The Indians were excellent trackers and soon caught up with the ungrateful Rangers. The two parties fought in a gulch near Mount Silver Heels.

Little is known about the battle. One of the Rangers

KENNETH JESSEN

died in the conflict, and his name was listed only as "John Smith." The Indians stripped "John Smith" of his clothes, but left his scalp. No trace was found of the other Rangers and it is presumed they escaped.

Doc Bailey of Montgomery was a jovial physician, but most of his practice was confined to staggering between one of the town's saloons and his cabin. He owned a drugstore and a shoe store in Montgomery. He was also an avid hunter. A few days after the Ute-Ranger battle, Doc was hunting along the base of Mount Silver Heels when he suddenly brought his horse to a stop. He could see a white object stretched out on the side of a rock, and it looked human. He rode over to the still form just as the others in his party arrived. Dismounting, Doc drew his hunting knife and tested its edge on his thumb. He remarked to his friends that he had always wanted a human head to dissect and study. Much to the horror of his companions, he sawed off the head of "John Smith," leaving the rest of the corpse to rot.

After he arrived back at his office, Doc Bailey got out a large pickle jar and submerged his trophy in pickling solution. So that all could see his prize possession, he placed the head in his office window. Needless to say, those passing by found the sight of the head in a pickle jar repulsive. It wasn't long before some citizen stole the head, placed it in a gunny sack, and dropped it into an abandoned mine shaft.

Long after "John Smith" and the story of the battle between the Rangers and the Ute Indians was forgotten, two miners purchased an old claim near the ghost town of Montgomery. The men pumped the water out of the shaft and began to clean out the debris to begin mining operations. While shoveling out the mud, one of them hit something round which was covered with rotting cloth. With the mud and cloth removed, the object clearly was a human skull. The discovery was a mystery; the abandoned shaft yielded no bones. Fortunately, an old timer remembered the story of Doc Bailey and solved the pickled skull mystery.

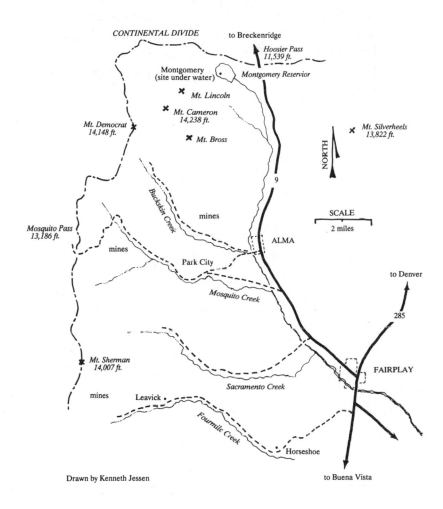

CONTINENTAL DIVIDE

to Breckenridge

Hoosier Pass
11,539 ft.

Montgomery
(site under water)

Montgomery Reservior

✗ *Mt. Lincoln*

✗ *Mt. Cameron*
14,238 ft.

Mt. Democrat
14,148 ft. ✗

✗ *Mt. Bross*

✗ *Mt. Silverheels*
13,822 ft.

NORTH

9

Buckskin Creek

mines

Mosquito Pass
13,186 ft.

SCALE

2 miles

mines

ALMA

Park City

to Denver

Mosquito Creek

285

✗ *Mt. Sherman*
14,007 ft.

FAIRPLAY

Sacramento Creek

mines

Leavick •

Fourmile Creek

Horseshoe

Drawn by Kenneth Jessen

to Buena Vista

STEEL SPIKE TURNED
TO SILVER

A general announcement was made in Denver that all businesses would be closed at noon on June 24, 1870. The occasion was one of the most significant moments in Denver history: the arrival of its first railroad, the Denver Pacific. On this day, Denverites were to witness not only the driving of the symbolic silver spike to complete the railroad, but the laying of the cornerstone for Union Station.

A long, colorful parade with men on black horses began its way from the Denver Masonic Hall at 15th Street and Larimer. It wound its way through the town to the railroad grounds at 19th Street and Wazee where the tracks of the Denver Pacific ended. The Masons were joined by the majority of Denver's 4,759 residents plus visitors from mining communities.

A special train, drawn by the locomotive "D. H. Moffat," brought 200 Masons south from Cheyenne over the newly laid track to join the festivities.

The mines in the Georgetown area had previously agreed to provide a spike made of pure silver for the ceremony. The spike was inscribed, "John Evans, President, June 24, 1870" on one side, and on the reverse side, "Georgetown to the Denver Pacific Railroad."

Billy Barton, proprietor of the Barton House in Georgetown, was given the responsibility of safely delivering the silver spike. When the day of the celebration approached, Barton and his friends left Georgetown for Denver. On their way through Golden, they stopped to quench their thirst. In the process, they got royally drunk. To keep their party alive, they needed to purchase more booze and pawned the spike. They then slept off their binge and the next day failed to rise in time to reach Denver for the ceremony.

At the time of the celebration, ex-Governor John Evans began with a speech while the locomotive slowly approached the end of the track. A band began to play, and the crowd pressed closer to witness John Evans driving the last spike. At the moment when Billy Barton was supposed to step forward and present the silver spike, there was silence. No Billy Barton, no Georgetown miners to represent him, and no spike.

General S. E. Browne, Attorney General for the Colorado Territory, was quick of wit and saw that something was wrong. He stooped down unnoticed and picked up a common steel spike. He quickly wrapped it in a piece of foil and handed it to Evans. Browne then exclaimed in a loud voice, "Here's the silver spike from Georgetown, with the compliments of the people of Clear Creek County." Evans held the spike in such a way that it could pass for silver.

Evans later redeemed the historic spike from the pawn shop. No word was recorded as to what action was taken against Billy Barton. The historic spike is now housed at the Colorado Historical Society.

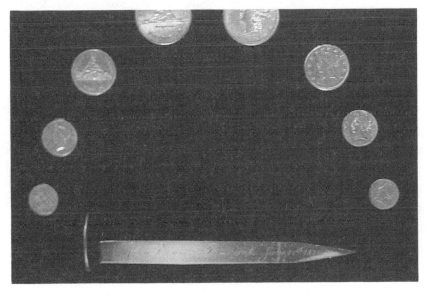

Ceremonial spike made of pure silver donated by the mines in Georgetown to commemorate the completion of the Denver Pacific in 1870. (Denver Public Library, Western History Department, negative F2229)

DUELING MADAMS

Possibly the West's only pistol duel between two female adversaries was fought on the night of August 25, 1877, in Denver's Olympic Gardens. Denver was a wide-open town during the 1870s, and this may be why Mattie Silks selected the Queen City to practice her profession. She was a madam and possessed a great talent for making money. Corteze D. Thompson, a gambler and runner, also became a resident of Denver. Cort and Mattie soon became good friends, and he began to depend on her money to make good his losses. In turn, she depended on his affection.

Mattie was described as a vest-pocket edition of the lovely Lily Langtry, famous stage personality of the period. Mattie's blue eyes and clear complexion complimented her blond curls. She was a little on the plump side which was in vogue at the time. Her clothing was purchased from the finest shops in Kansas City. As far as her taste, however, it bordered on the lurid, but fit her profession quite well.

All of Mattie's dresses had two pockets. In the left one she carried her coins, and in the right one, she toted a small pistol with ivory grips. The gun was a gift from Cort (using Mattie's money to purchase the weapon). In 1871, Mattie claimed that the famous gunfighter, Wild Bill Hickok, trained her in marksmanship. At the time, Mattie was operating a sporting house in Abilene, Texas, while Hickok served as town marshal.

Cort was Mattie's man. He was a Texan who spoke with a soft southern accent and claimed to have served with Quantrell's Raiders at the close of the Civil War. A brace of pistols was concealed inside his hip pockets. Cort was slender, of medium build, and had sandy blond hair. His mustache was kept neat in upturned curls typical of the day.

When he was racing, Cort wore pink tights and star-

*Mattie Silks was just 29 years old when she made history
by engaging in a duel with rival madam Kate Fulton. Mattie
claimed Wild bill Hickok trained her in marksmanship.*
(Colorado Historical Society, negative F-32942)

spangled blue running shorts. He also wore his assort-
ment of medals across his striped racing jersey. It should
be noted that he won a number of races despite the fact
that his training diet consisted of choice bourbon. As for
earning a living, Cort simply didn't believe in the work
ethic. His basic philosophy was to maintain a work-free
status by leaching off Mattie.

Kate Fulton, another Denver madam, was one of Cort's
admirers and attended his foot races. Kate's place of business was at 449 Holladay Street (now Market Street) in
Denver while Mattie's establishment was just down the
street at 501. The two were competitors in a sense.

After a win by Cort at the fairgrounds in August, 1877,
Mattie used the proceeds of her winnings to invite her
friends to a champagne jubilee at the Olympic Gardens
(also called the Denver Park) located just outside of the
Denver city limits on the west bank of the South Platte
River. It was the kind of place that drew the following
comment by the *Denver Times*, "...no woman who does not
desire to risk her reputation and perhaps her honor should
be willing to be seen there." It had a pavilion in a grove of
cottonwood trees and included a museum of freaks, a museum of ore samples, and a small zoo. Beer from the Denver Brewing Company was the primary beverage, and it was
the hangout for the town's "sporting" crowd.

At the party, Mattie's guests included Kate Fulton as
well as other Holladay Street proprietors. There were con
artists, faro bankers, card sharks, and many of Denver's
trollops.

As the evening wore on, something touched off a bitter
quarrel between Mattie and Kate. It could have been over
Kate's advances to Cort, or Cort could have turned his

attention toward Kate. In any event, the belligerent madams felt that only a duel to the death could settle their differences. Mattie selected Cort as her second; Kate chose a gambler named Sam Thatcher.

The party left the pavilion for a grove of trees on the bank of the river. As thirty paces were stepped off, it is likely that Denver's sporting element made book on the outcome.

Mattie, just 29 years old at the time, boasted of her marksmanship as the madams marched to their positions. Pistols were held ready, and the two women stood facing away from each other. At the count of three, they turned and fired. Amid the smoke and the noise, a scream penetrated the night air. Cort Thompson grabbed his neck and fell to the ground. Neither Mattie nor Kate were wounded. Blood spouted from between Cort's fingers as Mattie put her smoking pistol back into her pocket. She rushed to his side, and fortunately, it was only a flesh wound. In time, Cort recovered fully and later married Mattie.

NOTE: There are several versions of this quarrel that are equally interesting. Some accounts say that Thompson stepped in during a fist fight between Mattie and Kate and struck Kate in the face, knocking her to the ground. Sam Thatcher is said to have intervened on Kate's behalf and was also knocked down. Thompson's friends then attacked Thatcher as Kate tried to protect him. She was kicked in the face, and her nose was broken. Thompson's pistol was knocked out of his hand. When Thompson was returning home in a hack, someone came up to the carriage and shot him in the neck presumably with his own gun. Kate Fulton fled to Kansas City the following morning and returned to Denver when things had cooled off.

Mattie Silks, shown at the far left, is pictured with one of her prize racing horses. The woman with her is unidentified. (Denver Public Library, Western History Department, negative F7780)

THE LOST LOCOMOTIVE

On the evening of May 21, 1878, a tramp was sleeping in a dugout near the tracks of the Kansas Pacific where it crossed Kiowa Creek east of Denver. It rained for days in the Denver area, but little rain fell near the small town of Kiowa (now named Bennett). A flood came down Kiowa Creek and started filling the tramp's dugout. It must have been quite a surprise because the creek usually contained only a trickle of water. The tramp hurried down the track to warn the section man of the flood. The section man arrived at the creek just in time to see the force of the debris-filled water wash the Kansas Pacific's trestle away. In the dark, however, it looked like the trestle was still in place as the rails and ties were left suspended between the bridge abutments.

The first section of east-bound freight train No. 8 was running late. As the section man hurried to set up a red lantern to stop the train, the headlight loomed through the darkness. The train sped past, and when the locomotive traveled out on the unsupported track, it plunged into the swirling water. The tender and eighteen cars followed and piled on top of one another. The caboose, along with six flat cars, remained on the track.

One of two brakemen was setting the brakes using the hand wheels on a flat car when he saw the locomotive disappear. He ran across the cars, jumping from car to car, to the end of the train. He warned the conductor in the caboose and jumped for his life. The conductor jumped with him, and both survived their fall. They headed down the track away from the trestle and flagged down the second section of freight train No. 8.

Both the engineer, John Bacon, and his fireman, Frank Selden, went down with their locomotive and were killed.

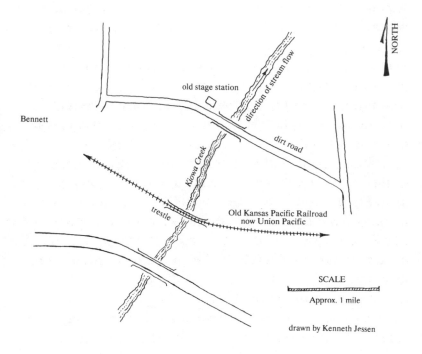

old stage station

direction of stream flow

NORTH

Bennett

dirt road

Kiowa Creek

Old Kansas Pacific Railroad
now Union Pacific

trestle

SCALE

Approx. 1 mile

drawn by Kenneth Jessen

John Piatt, a railroad employee, also perished in the wreck. Bacon and Selden were married to sisters, and both men lived in Denver. Piatt was on his way to a new job as a cook in Hugo.

By dawn the water subsided, and only the scattered remains of seven cars could be seen lying in the creek bed. A hobo was riding in one of the box cars that plunged off the abutment. He was found holding onto the top of the car and waiting for someone to come to his rescue. Frank Selden's body was found near what was left of the locomotive's cab a mile and a half downstream. John Piatt's body was also recovered in the same general area. The body of John Bacon could not be located. On Sunday, May 26, a special train ran from Denver to Kiowa piloted by the railroad's superintendent. It carried hundreds of members of the Brotherhood of Locomotive Engineers to search for his remains. After spending all day, Bacon's body was found seven miles from the trestle. The following day, all of the locomotives on the Kansas Pacific system were decked in mourning to honor the three employees lost in the tragedy.

To allow resumption of traffic, a shoo-fly was constructed around the site. The shoo-fly ran down the east bank on a steep nine percent grade, across the creek bed, and up the west bank on a six percent grade. A single locomotive could handle only eleven cars at a time. Construction of a new trestle began soon after the accident.

An immense amount of effort was expended to salvage as much equipment as possible, especially the $18,000 locomotive. Records indicate the engine was Number 51, had a 4-6-0 wheel arrangement, and weighed nearly forty tons. Cribbing was constructed in a forty-foot square, and a portable steam-powered pump was used to keep water and sand out of the excavation. The metal portions of some cars were recovered. Work continued for six weeks or more, and the tender was finally located. In a final effort to locate the lost locomotive, a long gas pipe was used to probe the creek bed. The Kansas Pacific apparently gave up trying to salvage its locomotive at this time. The water-sand mixture may have formed quicksand, allowing the heavy engine to settle to bedrock as much as fifty feet below the creek's surface.

Interest in the lost locomotive was rekindled in 1978 by Beth Sagstetter in an article that appeared in *Empire Magazine (Denver Post)*. Howard Starkel, a psychic, was invited by best-selling novelist, Clive Cussler (author of *Raise the Titanic* and *Night Probe*), in 1982 to use his psychic powers to tell what may have happened on that dark night so long ago. As Howard walked the creek bed toward the site of the old railroad bridge (now replaced by a steel span), he was given the names of the men who perished more than a century before. Howard presumably lacked prior knowledge of the incident and did not know why he was driven to the site. He commented how two of the men were in a confined space (maybe the locomotive cab) and how the third man was in the open (maybe on one of the cars). He felt that heat was involved and related that a bridge washed out. The psychic also said there were two explosions and that the locomotive jack-knifed after it hit the water. He pointed out where he thought the final resting place of the locomotive was today.

Clive Cussler advertised for volunteers to help him look for the lost locomotive in late 1988. On January 7 and 8, 1989, Clive and his National Underwater and Marine

Agency searched a small portion of the area with a magnetometer near the present-day bridge over Kiowa Creek.

About 200 spectators milled about the area. Cussler called off the search Sunday afternoon after having found nothing which could be positively identified as belonging to the wreck.

This renewed interest brought out several more facts about the wreck site. It is obvious that the railroad made a new and deeper cut leading up to Kiowa Creek. The new cut is about 15 feet downstream from the old cut. The railroad also added a substantial amount of fill over the years to raise the roadbed far above the flood plane. This means that the present-day bridge may not be where the original trestle was located. It also means that the fill may have buried the wreck even deeper than the silt from the creek. In addition, the state hydrologist pointed out that the creek has shifted as much as a mile side-to-side based on aerial photographs.

To dispel the legend of the lost locomotive of Kiowa Creek, Colorado Railroad Museum Director Bob Richardson did some research. Engine No. 51 was not lost at all, but was rebuilt in August, 1881. According to his records, its number was changed to 1026 in 1885. In 1886, No. 1026 remained on the railroad's inventory, but was listed in "poor condition." The financially troubled Kansas Pacific would have moved mountains to get their engine back. It is likely that the locomotive was retrieved at a later date when the creek bed was dry. Keep in mind that the sand was still saturated with water during the first attempt to find No. 51.

The locomotive shown above was quite similar to the type lost by the Kansas Pacific Railroad at Kiowa Creek. (Kenneth Jessen collection)

Novelist Clive Cussler searching for the lost locomotive of Kiowa Creek using a magnetometer. (photograph by Kenneth Jessen)

Modern steel bridge over Kiowa Creek near the town of Bennett. This bridge is near the site of the 1878 wreck where the locomotive, tender, and eighteen cars from east-bound train No. 8 piled into the creek bed. The engineer, fireman and a railroad employee perished in the accident. (photograph by Kenneth Jessen)

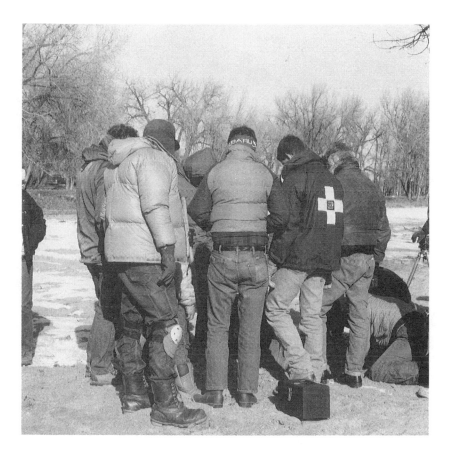

Volunteers digging in January, 1989, for the Kansas Pacific locomotive thought to be buried in the creek bed. (photograph by Kenneth Jessen)

BABY TOSSED INTO BLIZZARD

Welch Nossaman carried mail under contract between Del Norte and the mining town of Summitville during the 1870s. In the winter months, the twenty-eight mile trip took two days to travel up and back to Summitville. One winter, a severe blizzard hit the high country, and snow began to drift at Summitville. The situation became life threatening, and the residents elected to evacuate the town. They headed down the toll road toward Del Norte and agreed to remain there until the weather improved.

The Trelores were a young couple attracted to the rugged life in a Colorado mining town. They had a dog and a six-month old child. During the hazardous trip down from Summitville in the blinding, blowing snow, the wagons became stalled in a snowdrift. Mr. Trelore feared that his family would lose their lives in the storm, and he prayed to God to save his family.

Mail carrier Welch Nossaman came to the rescue and got the mules unhitched from the stalled wagons. He knew that the mules could make it through the deep snow by walking single file and by breaking a trail for them. The residents, including the Trelores, were placed on the backs of the animals, and the wagons were abandoned.

When the party arrived at the tollhouse at the base of the descent from Summitville, a big fire was built to warm everyone. After about half an hour, Mrs. Trelore realized that no one in the party had her young child and asked, "Where is my baby?"

Nossaman responded to the distraught mother, "Didn't you bring it out with you?"

She related how she had handed her child to the mule skinner, Dan Hoover. Nossaman immediately left the tollhouse to face the blizzard once again to find Hoover. He went to the stable and said to Hoover, "Dan, what did you do with Mrs. Trelore's baby?"

He responded, "I throwed it up in front of Joe Simmons on a mule."

Nossaman found Joe Simmons at the nearby water hole and asked, "Joe, what did you do with Mrs. Trelore's baby?"

He said he never brought a baby down from where the wagons were left. Nossaman told how Dan Hoover remembered wrapping the child up in bedding and throwing it up to him to place ahead of his saddle on the mule. When Joe was asked what he did with the roll of bedding, he responded, "Oh, a mule got down up there off the trail, and I dumped it off a mile or two above here. I thought we could go back and get the bedding if we needed it. I just left it laying there."

Nossaman promptly put on his snowshoes and faced the piercing cold. He went up the trail and eventually found a roll of bedding beside the trail. When he unwrapped the bedding, he found the baby dry and warm. He brought it down to the tollhouse. Mrs. Trelore, who became frantic over the loss of her only child, was very relieved. Her next question was, "Where's the dog?"

To that, Nossaman said he would not attempt another trip back to the wagons and that the dog would have to fend for itself. The next day some of the men returned to the wagons knowing the families would be safe in the warmth of the tollhouse. The dog was found buried under the snow and quite alive.

The blizzard trapped twenty to twenty-five people at the tollhouse. Almost all the bedding was in the wagons, and there was no food. The nearest place to get something to eat was eight miles away. The Trelores had their winter

Summitville as it looked in 1989. (photograph by Kenneth Jessen)

supplies in one of the wagons including bread, coffee, canned goods, and a quarter of beef. Mr. Trelore made his way back to his wagon to recover some of his food for his family. He never offered to divide his supplies with the others stranded in the tollhouse, including Nossaman. Selfishness of this sort was unusual during the settlement of the West.

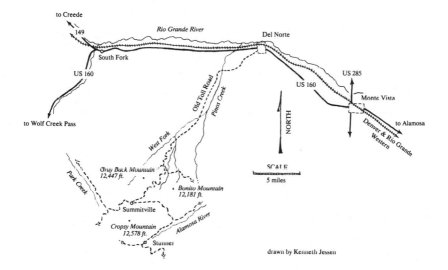

drawn by Kenneth Jessen

A COLORADO CACTUS TRAGEDY

During the 1870s, one of the trail riders for the Iliff Cattle Ranch in northeastern Colorado had just finished his lonely evening meal at a line cabin when his two dogs began barking. The cowboy knew that only Indians would upset his dogs to such an extent. He quickly barred the door and waited for a fight with the Indians or for a friendly visit.

The cabin was built with logs chinked with clay, and the Indians quickly went to work picking out the chinking and shooting through the cracks. The cowboy extinguished the candle and covered the coals in the fireplace with ashes. This made the room completely dark. He also removed his boots so he could move about quietly.

The shooting stopped, and before long, he noticed a few small sparks in the fireplace. He looked up the chimney just as the Indians dropped a bag of black powder down onto the coals. The explosion was immediate and sent the cowboy flying into the middle of the room. It also set the cabin on fire.

After recovering from the impact of the explosion, the cowboy grabbed his revolver and cartridge belt and ran out the back door. The Indians, of course, were expecting him. As he ran, he fired to either side, which kept them at bay.

The nearest settlement was ten miles away across a cactus flat. Barefoot, he ran as fast as he could to keep ahead of the Indians. He could hear them clearly, but they gave up the chase in the middle of the flat. He saw a settlement in the distance, but when he tried to walk, the many cactus spines in his feet forced him to crawl. Finally, he reached civilization at ten o'clock the following morning and was taken to the town of Evans to be treated. His hands, feet, arms, and legs were thickly covered with spines, and some of the spines had penetrated to the bone. A fever accompanied the great pain. The suffering cowboy was transferred to Cheyenne by train where he passed away a few days later.

His name was not recorded.

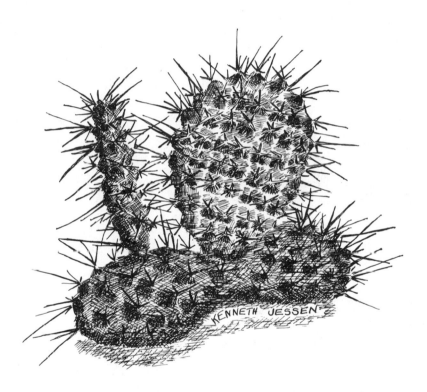

COUSIN JACKS

Cornwall, England, a small peninsula at the southwestern tip of Britain, was considered the home of the finest hard rock miners in the world. They mined tin and smelted it with copper to produce bronze. By the mid-1800s, the mines became so deep that it was no longer economical to continue operations. At that time, the Cornish men began to emigrate to other countries, including the United States.

Many of these fine miners were attracted to Colorado to help strengthen the state's mining economy. The Cornish miners brought their unique mannerisms, superstitions, and peculiar speech patterns with them. Especially noticeable was their way of adding an "h" sound at the beginning of words that had no "h," then leaving out the "h" sound where it should be. This was combined with other uniquely Cornish speech patterns. They had the habit of adding "you" after a statement. When asked how they were, they might answer, "Some grand you." They also called everyone by some endearing term such as, "My son" or "My beauty." Using "thee" for "you," they might inquire, " 'Ow are thee gettin' on there, my son?"

The Cornish became known as "Cousin Jacks" at the Colorado mining camps. Their talent as miners was exceptional, and when a mine foreman was impressed with his Cornish miner, he would ask if there were any others like him back in Cornwall. The Cornishman would usually know of other miners wanting to leave the old country and might answer, "My cousin Jack be a very good miner and 'ee should like a new job." The miners reasoned that foremen would be more apt to accept another member of the miner's family; where in fact, the "Cousin Jack" the miner had in mind might not be related at all. Because the men were known as "Cousin Jacks," it seemed fitting that the

Cornish women were known as "Cousin Jennies."

Some of the mining camp saloons offered a free drink to the first patron of the day. On a very cold, snowy morning, two "Cousin Jacks" arrived simultaneously at the door of a saloon with this particular offer to entice early drinking customers. The owner gave both a free drink. The drink warmed their souls after their brisk walk from home and was so fine that the Cornishmen decided to buy another.

As was their custom, they alternated paying for the drinks, and so it went on through the morning. Naturally, the more they consumed, the more they thought of facing the cold walk to the mine, and a long day underground became less attractive. The two men debated on whether to go to work and couldn't arrive at any conclusion. One of them came up with an idea to solve this dilemma and said, "Pardner, I'll tell thee what we'll do. We shall go out and throw a rock, and if 'ee stays up, we shall go to work!"

One "Cousin Jack" was forced to help his wife with a boarding house and bemoaned the high cost of food in the mining camp. To get away from the house for a while, he decided to try a brand new saloon. A stuffed owl was mounted in back of the bar as a novelty item. The first thing that caught the eye of the Cornishman was that owl. Apparently he had never seen this type of bird in the old country and asked the bartender, "Ere, my Son, 'ow much is that flat-face chicken up there?"

The bartender replied, "That's no flat-face chicken, that's a owl."

Misunderstanding the reply, the Cornishman retorted sharply, "I don't care 'ow hold 'ee is, 'ee's good enough for boarders!"

As more Cornish miners joined the ranks of the mining

Owl at the bar in South Park City. (photograph by Kenneth Jessen)

camps, an expression came forth: "Wherever there is a hole in the earth, you will find a Cornishman at the bottom of it."

One Colorado Cornish miner claimed he worked so high in altitude that he could hear the angels sing and down so deep in the earth that he could hear the Chinese doing their dishes.

Methodist Bishop Donald H. Tippett came in contact with many Cornish miners and lived in Central City. He recalled that the camp was so crowded that the miners were forced to sleep three to a bed. Whenever one of them wanted to turn over he shouted, "Ready!" The second man would repeat, "Ready." The third man would then say, "Turn." All three would then turn over in unison.

One night three Cornish miners were rather drunk and wandered into the St. James Methodist Church during a revival meeting. Finding a pew at the back, the trio sat down just as the evangelist was warming the crowd up with a hymn. The verse went, "The Judgment Day is Coming, Are You Ready?" The preacher repeated in a loud voice, "Are You Ready?" The miners found it irresistible and joined in with a shout, "Turn!"

The Cornish miners had many superstitions and strongly believed that a woman in a mine was bad luck. Whistling in a mine could also bring bad luck. Greatly feared were the "knockers." They were big-headed, small-eyed, wide-mouthed, evil spirits that could vanish in a puff of smoke. A "knocker" stood about two feet tall, and they were believed to be the spirits of dead miners. They wore tiny miner's boots and colorful shirts. The "knockers" used small hammers and picks to torment the Cornish miners while they were at work. It was very bad luck to run across one of these creatures in a dark mine passage. Mine explosions and cave-ins were blamed by the Cornish on the "knockers."

Colorado Historical Society

THE ADVENTURES
OF BALAAM

Sergeant O'Keefe arrived in Colorado Springs, January, 1876, to man the station operated by the U.S. Signal Corps at the top of 14,110-foot Pikes Peak. His job at this windy, cold outpost was to operate the weather station established two years before. O'Keefe, however, became famous not for the dry statistics of meteorological phenomena, but rather for the astounding experiences he claimed to have had on the peak. Using the telegraph line from the peak to Colorado Springs far below, O'Keefe had a ready audience for adventures with his mule, Balaam. The American public seemed willing to believe the incomprehensible. O'Keefe became the master of the hoax when his story of an attack by mountain rats appeared in the May 25, 1876, edition of the *Colorado Springs Gazette* and repeated in the *Rocky Mountain News*. (O'Keefe, by the way, claimed that his infant daughter was eaten by the voracious rats and even carried this hoax to the point of having funeral services on the summit of Pikes Peak.)

On a cold February morning in 1880, O'Keefe was riding toward the summit on the back of Balaam, and they encountered a large number of black-tailed deer near Mennehaha Falls. So large was the herd that O'Keefe could not get through, and he estimated its size at 127 animals. He claimed it took over one hour and forty minutes just for the deer to pass a given point on the trail.

Armed with a .32 caliber Smith and Wesson revolver, O'Keefe shot seventeen deer to supply the station. He gathered up the dead deer, tied their tails together, and slung the mass over Balaam's neck. The journey up the trail continued without incident until they reached a mountain of snow piled across the trail. Sergeant O'Keefe urged his veteran Government mule up the snowdrift which he

estimated to be twenty-eight feet tall. At the top,
O'Keefe dismounted and saw nothing ahead but even larger
snowbanks. He felt it would be useless to continue and
decided to head back to Colorado Springs. Turning to step
back into the saddle, he discovered Balaam had disappeared. He retraced his steps through the snowdrift and
after a good hour, reached the other side. He hoped to find
some trace of Balaam and much to his chagrin, he found
the mule at the bottom of a deep ravine. The black-tailed
deer were scattered from the top to the bottom, and the
mule was lying on his back with his feet in the air. The
Sergeant struggled down the ravine and rescued Balaam by
helping him back to the trail. The deer were gathered up
and placed on the saddle.

Soon, O'Keefe and Balaam reached a secluded part of
the trail in a deep forest where they were attacked by six
ravenous mountain lions. In order to save his life and that
of his mule, O'Keefe was forced to cast the deer carcasses
to the lions. The seventeen deer, however, failed to satisfy
the appetites of the lions and they continued to stalk him.
Eventually, O'Keefe managed to reach the safety of his
office in Colorado Springs by eight o'clock in the evening.

In November, O'Keefe corrected one of the facts con-
cerning his adventure on Pikes Peak. He admitted he
feared his close friends would think he exaggerated a bit.
O'Keefe told the local newspaper that there were actually
only 126 black-tailed deer and that the 127th animal had a
white tail!

In December, 1880, Sergeant O'Keefe and his mule,
Balaam, were the center of attention in front of the U.S.
Signal Corps office in Colorado Springs. As a reporter
from the local paper approached, O'Keefe was heard to

Sergeant O'Keefe and his trusty mule, Balaam carrying black-tailed deer down Pikes Peak.

remark, "Gentlemen, you can laugh at that mule all you please, but he is endowed with better instincts and has got more of a history to back him than any one of you." Balaam, standing by O'Keefe, reacted with a long bray. The mule, by the way, was gray, stood fourteen hands high, and showed the unmistakable signs of having been subjected to many hardships.

O'Keefe boasted that Balaam was the first mule to conquer Pikes Peak and breathe the breath of life above 14,000 feet. For seven years, Balaam was used to haul people and supplies to the top and according to O'Keefe's records, made no less than 1,924 trips or an equivalent of 40,960 miles. In the process, Balaam wore out 560 sets of shoes or about a ton of iron.

According to O'Keefe, the origin of the mule's name is quite curious. During the first summer O'Keefe was in Colorado Springs, he got into a heated argument with Cherokee Charley, a notorious desperado. Cherokee Charley insisted that O'Keefe was an Irishman, not an Italian as the Sergeant claimed. After a fierce fist fight, both were arrested and tossed into the Colorado Springs jail. O'Keefe could not gain access to his government allowance to post bail. He was forced to pawn his mule in order to "bail'em" out which is how the mule got the name "Balaam." (The name actually is that of an Old Testament prophet who is reproached by the ass he is riding.)

An associate of O'Keefe's, J.K. Sweeney, related to the press about the time Balaam escaped and how efforts to recapture the animal proved useless. It seemed that the government cut the rations for all of its mules and Sweeney knew that, "...the mule would make a bold, bad break for liberty some day." The cut in food produced what Sweeney described as mutiny in the mule's eyes. There is no doubt that Balaam planned his escape very carefully.

When Sergeant O'Keefe was on his way up Pikes Peak, he stopped for the night at a cabin, unsaddled the mule, and placed him in the barn. Following Government orders, he did not give Balaam his normal supply of oats. As O'Keefe was about to settle into his blankets for the evening, he heard a series of distressing brays from Balaam. Thinking that the animal was under attack from wild animals, O'Keefe hurried to the barn. As he opened the door, Balaam sped past and down the mountain to freedom. The mule had been waiting by the door and had outwitted O'Keefe. The Sergeant swore that if he ever captured the animal, he would cremate him and mail his ashes to the Smithsonian as a specimen of the ashes from what O'Keefe claimed was the active volcano on Pikes Peak!

O'Keefe immediately telegraphed Sweeney and told him to saddle up the other mule, Kit, and to recapture Balaam. Soon after this message, the telegraph line went dead and the weather station was now cut off from Colorado Springs. Sweeney commented, "I'll bet my month's salary that Balaam realized over a week ago that he would be called upon to assist in repairing the telegraph line and here we are in a fine predicament without a mule that had an electrical education." This, of course, reflected on Balaam's legendary ability to find a broken wire. The next morning, Sweeney had no luck in finding the fault in the line with Kit, the poor unintelligent, un-intellectual and uneducated mule.

In the meantime, Balaam joined a band of seven wild horses with manes and tails so long they dragged on the ground. Even more striking, the horses were jet black and the manes and tails were pure white. Sweeney found Balaam among his new associates, and not even an ear of corn could entice the renegade mule within 800 yards.

Sweeney had to search hard for Balaam the next morning. He was no longer with the wild horses. Sweeney came up over a rise and there stood Balaam, fighting three full-grown mountain lions. At this point, Sweeney didn't care who won and simply watched. Balaam held his own and would kick with his forefeet when the lions approached from the front and with his powerful hind feet if attacked from the rear. With these vigorous kicks, Balaam killed two lions and the third retreated.

Thinking the mule was exhausted, Sweeney concluded he could easily capture the animal, but upon the first attempt, Balaam dashed down a deep ravine and out of sight. Sweeney skinned the two lions and headed back to Colorado Springs. Eventually Balaam was captured and returned to service for the U.S. Signal Corps.

O'Keefe's tall tales of his highly exaggerated experiences on Pikes Peak were widely published. His fame, however, led to his resignation which may have been forced by his employer. Mountain rats and volcanoes on Pikes Peak enriched Colorado history to be sure, but his reputation as a prevaricator was an embarrassment to the U.S. Signal Corps. In any event, O'Keefe was honored at a banquet in Colorado Springs in December, 1881. As reported by Stanley Wood, O'Keefe related yet another yarn about his trusty mule Balaam. By this time in the evening, his speech may have been slurred by strong drink, but according to official reports of this event, only mineral water from Manitou Springs was served.

It happened dthis way: Balaam dthe government mule, and meself were ascending the Peak when all at once we were attacked by a ravenous mountain lion. Oi threw a bit on him wid me carbine, me intention was to shoot him (the lion) in dthe oi. Dthis intention failed for Oi missed him altogether. He leaped upon me and dracked me from the moule and we struggled togither on the ground. Oi drew me revolver, me intention failed for the pistol missed fired. Balaam was an interested specthator av dthe struggle, and seeing me loik to get dthe worst ov it, he opened his spacious mouth and with one snap, bit dthe lion's head clean off and swallowed it. Ov coorse afther dthat, it made no difference how good me intention was to shoot him in the oi.

History failed to record Balaam's fate after O'Keefe left his post. At the time of his death in 1895, O'Keefe was employed by the Denver Fire Department and was sta tioned on Colfax Avenue.

A CURE FOR
TALLOW MOUTH

Life was hard in mining towns like Leadville. Little medical care was available, and at an elevation of 10,152 feet above sea level, it was difficult to stay warm in drafty mining shanties. Tall tales originated under these adverse conditions, but they were passed on to others as the absolute truth. For example, newcomers to Leadville were told that in 1877, meat became so scarce during the harsh winter, that all the men could find to eat was venison and fried potatoes. They ate so much venison fat, or tallow, that it built up on the roofs of their mouths. This substantially cut down on conversation, and the miners only talked when it was essential. Eventually the tallow became so thick that the men couldn't even taste coffee or whiskey.

Many solutions were proposed and tried. According to the miners, the most effective was to cover the victim's head with pine knots and needles. Pine pitch was used to hold the mess together. Someone then set the heap on fire, and as the heat became intense, it melted the tallow from the roof of the miner's mouth and restored the victim's taste. No cure such as this was entirely free of side effects, and in this case the cure caused permanent baldness. By the end of the terrible winter of 1877, it was said that 97 percent of Leadville's miners were bald.

In the middle of the following spring, a gentleman from Kentucky reached Leadville and noticed the plight of the bald miners. He was in the hair tonic business and immediately began to manufacture his product from potatoes. Tallow mouth victims readily purchased his product.

One rainy summer evening, he was headed to town from his cabin with four jugs of hair tonic. He held on to one in each hand and tucked one under each arm. On the way, he was forced to cross a log over a small creek that emptied into the Arkansas River. He lost his balance momentarily on the slippery log and dropped the jugs under his arms. The two jugs broke when they hit the rocks in the stream.

Local fishermen downstream from the hair tonic maker's cabin reported that they switched fishing methods. Instead of using a rod and reel, they stuck a red, white, and blue barber's pole in the bank, put on a white coat, waved a magazine in one hand, and carried a pair of hair scissors in the other hand. When a fisherman called out "Next!," a fine hair-covered trout jumped out of the water to get a trim. In a short time, fishermen reached their limit using these tonsorial lures.

**BEFORE AND AFTER THE CURE FOR
TALLOW MOUTH**

*THE GREAT
ROCK WALL*

High on the mountainside, near the gravel road leading up Ohio Creek north of Gunnison, stands a large rock wall. It sits on a steep talus slope and spans the gap between two cliffs. Upon close examination, it is apparent that the wall was never completed as evidenced by the large steps along its top. About eight feet thick, the wall is composed of hand-fitted rock laid without mortar. The wall stands about 45 feet above its base, and if it had been completed, it would have been 60 feet high.

At either end of the wall are shelves cut into the cliffs which form a constant grade headed toward Ohio Pass. Downgrade and away from the pass, the grade ends abruptly in an aspen grove at the edge of another talus slope. Piles of rock, however, mark the route across the slide. By connecting completed portions of the grade, it is apparent that the jeep road directly below the wall is part of a giant loop used to gain altitude.

The purpose for this great wall is not clear to many, but for Colorado historians the great rock wall is no mystery. It is part of a railroad grade and represents the last attempt by the narrow gauge Denver, South Park & Pacific to reach westward into Utah. The wall is a tribute to the tenacity of its builders, yet a monument to the failure of the railroad to attain its goal. It stands above conifer forests and rich meadows filled with wild flowers to remind us of ambitious times during the 1880s to develop the state's resources.

The Denver, South Park & Pacific began construction in Denver in 1873 and reached Morrison the following year. From this humble beginning, the Denver, South Park & Pacific grew to become Colorado's largest narrow gauge system with 335 miles of track. It headed south out of Denver, west through the Platte River Canyon, and over

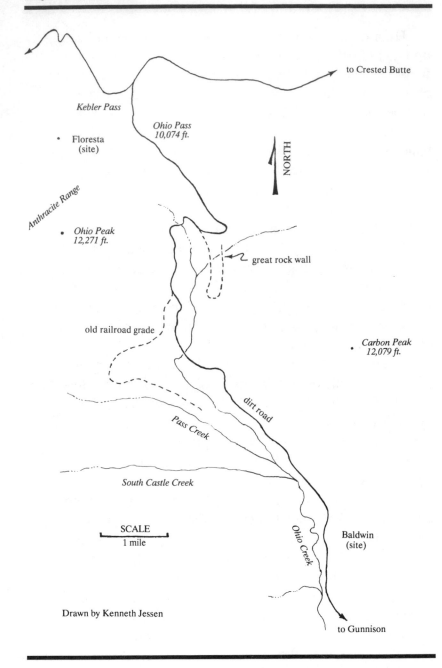

to Crested Butte

Kebler Pass

Ohio Pass
10,074 ft.

NORTH

• Floresta
(site)

Anthracite Range

• *Ohio Peak*
12,271 ft.

great rock wall

old railroad grade

• *Carbon Peak*
12,079 ft.

dirt road

Pass Creek

South Castle Creek

SCALE
1 mile

Ohio Creek

Baldwin
(site)

Drawn by Kenneth Jessen

to Gunnison

Kenosha Pass. It crossed South Park through Fairplay
and, via Trout Creek Pass, reached Buena Vista in the
Arkansas River Valley. From there, it went up Chalk
Creek Canyon through the mining town of St. Elmo, then
through the Alpine Tunnel at an elevation of 11, 523 feet.
From there, the line dropped down Quartz Creek through
Pitkin to Gunnison.

The Denver, South Park & Pacific reached Gunnison in
1882, and the railroad announced plans to continue construction to the west. Grading began up Ohio Creek in
January, 1882, with plans to go over Ohio Pass and down
Anthracite Creek on the west side of Kebler Pass. The
great rock wall probably was built during the spring. The
following year the rails of the Denver, South Park & Pacific
reached Castleton, 15 miles north of Gunnison. The line
was extended another three miles to serve the New Baldwin
Mine. This coal mine was as close as the Denver, South
Park & Pacific trains came to the Utah state line.

In 1883, the Denver, South Park & Pacific abandoned
its construction up Ohio Creek in favor of an easier grade
via the Gunnison River and Slate Creek to Crested Butte.
This route, paralleling the rival narrow gauge Denver &
Rio Grande, was to pass through Crested Butte, but no
grading was ever completed.

The cave-in of the Alpine tunnel closed the Denver,
South Park & Pacific's route to Gunnison in 1888. The
tunnel was reopened in 1895, but because of the expense of
operating at high altitude, the tunnel was closed permanently in 1910. The Denver, South Park & Pacific turned
over the operation of its spurs north of Gunnison to the
Denver & Rio Grande. The last train puffed up Ohio
Creek to the New Baldwin Mine in 1952, and two years

later the track was removed.

The railroad grades of both the Denver, South Park & Pacific and the Denver & Rio Grande are now overgrown with vegetation and marked by rotting ties. The trestles were removed and salvaged for lumber, and most of the water tanks and depots are gone. The enormous multistory, coal mine buildings were turned into scrap metal. The one enduring feature, however, is the great rock wall of Ohio Creek.

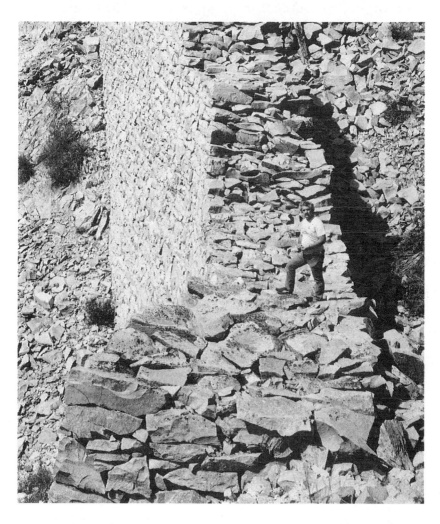

Eldon Ashbaugh standing on the partially completed wall.
(photograph by Kenneth Jessen)

BOSCO'S BAGGAGE

The narrow gauge Rio Grande Southern served many Colorado mining towns including Placerville, Telluride, Durango, Ridgeway, and Rico. Telluride was reached by a branch of the Rio Grande Southern which left the main line at Vance Junction. About a half mile away lived Colonel Vance. He was a bachelor who stayed in a small cabin and was periodically drunk. He would go on a binge every payday.

On one particular day, Colonel Vance came to the depot at Vance Junction following a serious drinking bout. After a brief visit, he ventured up the lush hillside catching big, green grasshoppers.

A snake charmer named Bosco had finished his show at Telluride and was on his way south to give another show at Rico. He had to transfer from the local Telluride train to the southbound train and was forced to wait at Vance Junction. He entered the depot with a suitcase full of snakes, but when his train arrived, Conductor Sanders would not allow the snakes on board. Bosco had to leave the suitcase in the office to be forwarded on the next southbound freight.

In the meantime, the Colonel was still on the hill above the depot catching grasshoppers when the agent called to him to come down. The agent wanted to surprise the Colonel with the contents of the suitcase. The Colonel was so hung over that when he saw the snakes he wasn't afraid and grabbed an armful of the serpents. The astonished agent watched as he scattered them all over the office area. Included were rattlers, water snakes, and dozens more. The agent spent the day sweeping snakes out of the Vance Junction depot. After the Colonel sobered up a little, it became clear to him what he had done, and he became scared stiff.

This unfortunate incident put Bosco temporarily out of business. He cursed at the conductor when he learned what had happened to his "performers." He returned to Vance Junction to salvage what he could, but some of the snakes already had gone off into the woods.

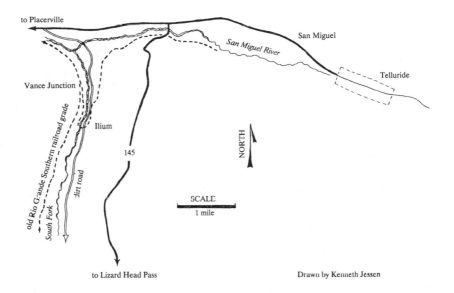

to Placerville

San Miguel

San Miguel River

Telluride

Vance Junction

old Rio Grande Southern railroad grade

Ilium

dirt road

South Fork

145

NORTH

SCALE
1 mile

to Lizard Head Pass

Drawn by Kenneth Jessen

MASKED MARRIAGE

The first pastor of the Presbyterian Church in Durango, Rev. James M. McFarland, held his position from 1881 to 1882. During his brief stay, he learned that outlaws as well as upstanding citizens of the area needed his services. One night at eleven o'clock, after the preacher had retired, there was a knock at his door. He told his visitor through the door that he had retired for the evening, but the visitor threatened to kick in the door unless it was opened. As the Reverend opened the door, a masked man holding a revolver and a five dollar bill greeted the pastor. The man said to Rev. McFarland, "Partner, I want to get married. I want you to attend the service. I will give you five minutes in which to dress and get ready to go with me to perform the ceremony."

The Reverend had no choice but to dress. He was escorted to a lonely spot along the Animas River. They were joined by two other men and after listening, the Reverend learned that the groom was without his bride. Friends and relatives of the prospective bride who lived nearby opposed the marriage and were prepared to shoot it out to protect her.

The masked prospective groom was determined to win his prize, and the men formed a battle line in preparation to storm the house if necessary. The Reverend was forced to march along. When the groom's party reached the house, its occupants were waiting. Somehow, violence was avoided, and the groom's party was allowed to enter the house.

At that time, Reverend McFarland was not ordained and had no legal right to perform the marriage ceremony. He would have been nervous under normal circumstances, but, finding himself amid an armed camp, could only

improvise: "Everybody in the house stand up - join
hands - faint heart never won fair lady, and a coward is not
worth a groat <sic>. Nevertheless, in the presence of these
everlasting mountains, and the great country of which we
form a part, and in accordance with God's word, whom He
hath joined together let no man put asunder, I now declare
you joined together as husband and wife. Be careful that
you do not both ever get mad at the same time. May you
live long and die happy. Amen."

Just as the Reverend uttered the Amen, one of the
groom's friends yelled, "Run, Partner." The party ran back
to the river bank and up on an adjoining bluff. Rev.
McFarland never learned what became of the couple he
joined. He later commented about this wedding ceremony,
"I am now satisfied that it has served a more sacred service
than some that I have since performed with more authority
and under infinitely more propitious conditions."

PIE OVEN CREATES TRAFFIC JAM

In March, 1881, some impatient Leadville bakers decided to move a huge pie oven over 12,095-foot Independence Pass to cash in on what was potentially a lucrative pie market in Aspen. The road over Independence Pass, however, was not complete, and only a trail existed over the upper portion of the pass.

The bakers purchased a large sled and secured the pie oven to the sled with ropes. A half-dozen jacks were used for motive power. As the trip up the pass progressed, the trail narrowed to the point where the sides of the oven caught on the rocks. This required the anxious bakers to excavate earth and rock from each side of the narrow trail to continue the trip over the pass. That night, the weary bakers slept in the oven and were haunted by the faint aroma of pastry.

A new difficulty arose the next morning as the spring tide of travelers followed the baker's oven over the pass to reach Aspen. The commercial freighters could not get their jacks and wagons around the large pie oven. They were in a hurry to get their goods to the new mining community, but had to resign themselves to follow the slow progress of the pie oven.

One freighter arrived behind the traffic jam and asked, "What's up?"

Another freighter answered, "A G-- D-- pie factory is blocking the road!"

"Well, why don't you push the --- thing off?"

To this, the second freighter replied, "Can't do it; it's too hell-fired big!"

The jam soon extended nearly a mile in back of the oven and consisted of many swearing, howling men.

The following summer, well after the busy bakers set up

their pie oven in Aspen, seventy-five men labored building the Independence Pass toll road along with many of the people in the small mining town of Independence. The toll road officially opened November 6, 1881, and it shortened the distance from Aspen to Leadville from around one hundred miles via Cottonwood Pass to sixty miles.

Traffic poured over Independence Pass, and the toll company kept a small army of men on hand to keep the road clear through the snowstorms. All through the winter, a solid double line of traffic moved in opposite directions over the new road.

The hairpin turns were eventually banked and broadened so that during the summer, stage coaches could descend with their teams at a full gallop. Dogs were sometimes used to run ahead of the stage coaches to warn the uphill traffic that a speeding coach was approaching.

Independence, Colorado, viewed from Colorado 82 over Independence Pass. This modern road follows the original toll road in most places. (photograph by Kenneth Jessen)

103

MAGNIFICENT FLYING MACHINES

Colorado was not without its inventors, especially in the area of flying machines. For example, the *Denver Republican* reported in 1888 that Charles H. Morgan of Gunnison invented an "improved" airship using flapping wings for propulsion. The invention even was featured in *Scientific American*.

Morgan's patented airship was listed as light, yet strong. It was roomy and, according to Morgan, could fly easily. He also claimed it was easy to maneuver. Constructed of a series of tubes running the length of the flying machine, the tubes were bent to assume a football shape. The purpose of the tubes was to hold compressed gas, while ribs formed the frame. The patent called for either a metal or silk skin over the frame to act as the airship's cover.

Part of the propulsion system took the form of bird's wings which were used to propel the ship upward and forward as they dipped and stroked through the air. The rudder was the shape of a fish tail and moved back and forth as the machine flew. The compressed gas was Morgan's real secret and was exhausted into chambers inside the ship. Valves were used to control the concentration of the gas and regulate the airship's altitude.

With the flapping, stroking, and release of gas, Morgan's airship would have been interesting in flight, but as far as is known, none ever was constructed.

Inventor George L. O. Davidson constructed a prototype flying machine of enormous proportions. Davidson lived in the Denver suburb of Montclair where he constructed his aircraft in 1907. This Scottsman claimed he discovered the correct theory for the law of flight. His machine was designed to fly from Chicago to New York City in three hours while carrying one hundred passengers.

"Gyroscopic rotary lifters" made of 110 eight-foot blades were supposed to allow the machine to fly. The lifters revolved horizontally on vertical shafts much like a helicopter. The shafts could be tilted to vary the amount of lift. Rudders fore and aft on the body of the machine were controlled by steering wheels. To power this machine, a pair of 50-horsepower steam engines was used. A million dollars was put up to construct the prototype and others like it, and in 1908, Davidson was ready to test his theory. The giant machine rose forty feet above Davidson's's backyard and exploded. Windows were broken for blocks around. The pilot suffered a broken leg, burns, and got a steel splinter in his right eye. This ended Davidson's dream.

In 1928, Jonathan Caldwell founded the Gray Goose Airways, which was coupled to Caldwell's innovative approach to flight. He, like Morgan, believed that aircraft were meant to fly like birds using moving wings. This was at the time when the accepted theory of flight was to use fixed wings lifted by the horizontal movement of air.

Caldwell tinkered away at his Denver shop while an aggressive sales staff of ten sold shares in the Gray Goose Airways. Caldwell was unable to produce a single successful design, and the public began to suspect that his inventions were nothing more than a scam. In 1931, Caldwell may have been forced to leave Denver. He moved to New Jersey, then to New York, next to Washington D.C. and to Maryland. In each location, once officials realized that he was more of a con artist than an inventor, stock sales were prohibited.

Although these inventions did not revolutionize aviation, they represent the creativity of pioneer Coloradoans.

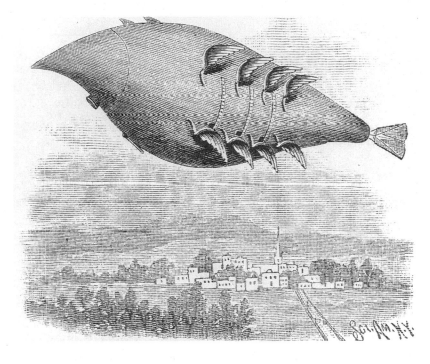

*Morgan's patented airship used structures which looked
like bird's wings to propel it forward. The rudder moved back
and forth much like a fish tail.* (Denver Public Library,
Western History Department, negative F13487)

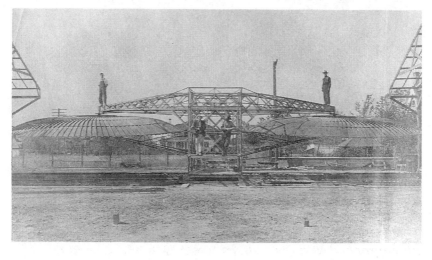

"Gyroscopic rotary lifters" on this steam-powered flying machine were supposed to allow it to fly. In 1908, the sixty foot machine did rise forty feet above the ground before it exploded. (Denver Public Library, Western History Department, negative F24222)

This is Jonathan Caldwell's motorcycle-powered aircraft photographed at an old airstrip near Denver. It used a flapping motion like a bird rather than a conventional fixed wing and propeller. This was just one of several designs for use by the Gray Goose Airways, but such a craft would hardly inspire confidence among potential customers. (Colorado Historical Society, negative F28449)

A DOUBLE-BARRELED THREAT

Lay, Colorado, in the remote northwestern part of the state, was once a military post. After U.S. soldiers moved the Ute Indians out of the state into Utah, the post at Lay was abandoned. Widow Mary A. Farnham, a spunky silver-haired lady, obtained the army barrack building where she operated the Lay post office. She also started a roadhouse, and it soon proved to be the best place to eat and stay in the area. It was kept spotless. The beds were free of bugs (unusual for a roadhouse in that part of the state), and the food was excellent. Cowboys rode extra dusty miles just to put their tired feet under the Widow Farnham's table.

As an extra bonus to the almost all male population in the area, Mary Farnham was very attractive. She was also straight-laced and wouldn't tolerate any fooling around. She didn't allow liquor on her premises or prostitutes brought in by the lonely cowboys.

In 1889, after transacting some ranching business in the area, Hi Bernard decided to ride over to a saloon about six miles from Lay. After getting drunk, he rode over to Lay and, on a whim, urged his horse right into the middle of Widow Farnham's kitchen. Not especially surprised by the intrusion, she took Bernard's entrance in stride. The widow stepped into an adjoining room and returned with a double-barreled shotgun. She calmly broke the breech and inserted a couple of shells. Even though he was intoxicated, Hi realized how serious these actions were and got out of the kitchen just as she fired. As he rode hard to get out of range, he fell from his horse into the sagebrush. With buckshot in the cantle of the saddle, his horse took off at a full gallop for safer places. Hi was forced to keep low and crawl through the sagebrush with Widow Farnham hunting for his hide.

Hi Bernard was suddenly quite sober and waited in the dark before daring to walk back to the saloon. He spent the night on the saloon's filthy floor behind the bar.

Later, to save what was left of his self-respect, Hi tendered money to buy out Mary Farnham. The widow was well established and held the position of postmistress. She refused to sell.

After the passage of six years and still quite ashamed of his behavior, Hi Bernard returned to Lay to apologize to that spunky lady. He rode into town, tied up his horse, and dropped by the post office. Before he could get his bearings, up popped Mary Farnham lugging her shotgun. He quickly ducked through the door and ran for all he was worth, zig-zagging through the sagebrush for the nearest cover. This was the second time Hi Bernard was forced to leave his horse behind in Lay to save his hide.

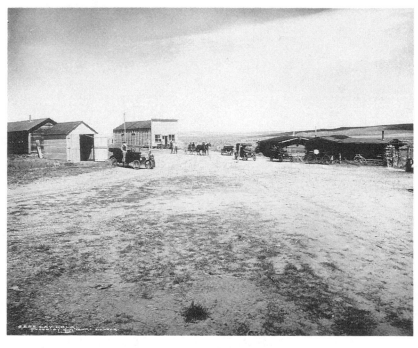

Lay, Colorado, located in the northwestern part of the state, is pictured here after the turn of the century. (Denver Public Library, Western History Department, negative McC2552)

THE SAN MIGUEL
FLUME

The story of one of the most spectacular engineering feats in the history of Colorado began during the 1880s when prospectors discovered a placer deposit of finely powdered gold on Mesa Creek Flats above the Dolores River four miles below its junction with the San Miguel River. The water flow from Mesa Creek was so small, however, that panning operations were restricted to the spring and early summer. Nearly every pan contained some gold flour, and it was believed that if more water could be brought into Mesa Creek Flats to support hydraulic mining, a fortune could be made.

This led to the construction of one of the most unique structures in Colorado history: a flume suspended on a vertical sandstone cliff high above the Dolores River and the San Miguel River.

Capitalists from St. Louis formed the Montrose Placer Mining Company. It was managed by Col. N. P. Turner, an experienced mining man who knew that the first task was to bring water into the area from the San Miguel River. The river was a dozen miles away, and Turner proposed to carry the water by a combination of a ditch and a flume.

Hydraulic mining utilizes large nozzles to wash the gold bearing gravel into a sluice for recovery of the gold dust. The water requirements for this type of mining are substantial. A sluice looks very much like a flume and is placed at an angle sufficient to allow gravel and sand to pass through. There are small boards called riffles nailed across the bottom of the flume from one side to the other to trap the sand which contains the heavier gold particles. At the beginning of each shift, the miner places a small amount of mercury in each riffle to amalgamate the gold particles. The gold is "soluble" in mercury. The gold and mercury amalgamation are recovered at the end of the shift and the gold is separated from the mercury. The mercury then is placed back in the riffles.

The water diversion project was started in 1889 and completed two years later. The intake point was on the San Miguel River near the present-day town of Uravan. The project required a flume eight miles long on the northern wall of the San Miguel Canyon, four feet deep and six feet wide to carry the necessary volume of water. The flume was supported by brackets embedded in the side of the vertical sandstone cliffs. The flume varied from 100 to 150 feet above the river bed and 250 to 500 feet below the rim of the gorge. This spectacular structure ran a mile and a half on the cliffs above the San Miguel River and six and a half miles on the canyon wall above the Dolores River.

The flume required a great deal of milled lumber. The Montrose Placer Mining Company set up a saw mill just across the state line in Utah to provide the lumber. Pine boards, two inches thick, were hauled by wagon to the construction site. In all, an estimated 1.8 million board-feet of lumber were used in this project.

To construct the flume, a flat car on a temporary track nailed into the flume was used. The flat car was equipped with a long crane at one end and a counter weight of rocks at the other end. Workmen were held over the canyon wall while they drilled holes in the sandstone for the iron brackets. After a bracket was in place, a section of flume was constructed. The tracks on the flume bed were advanced, the flat car was pushed ahead, and the next bracket was installed. In some places, men were lowered over the side of the rim to drill the holes and install the brackets. The grade of the flume was held to a steady six feet, ten inches

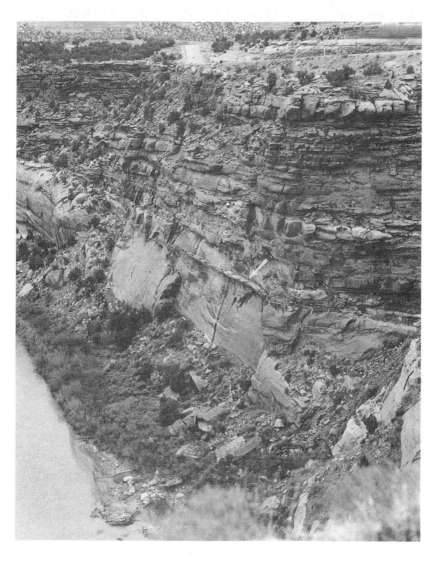

*The rotting remains of the San Miguel flume still cling to
the sandstone cliffs. The flume can be viewed from Colorado
141 near Uravan.* (photograph by Kenneth Jessen)

per mile.

Men were paid $2.50 a day, and about twenty-five were assigned to work on the flume.

To get the milled lumber to the flume, some was hoisted from the canyon floor with ropes. Other times, the lumber was lowered over the canyon rim. Some material was floated by barge down the river to the construction site.

The cost of the great flume was over $100,000, and the project was completed in the early summer of 1891. Water flowed the entire distance in fine shape and was delivered at the rate of 80,000,000 gallons per day.

The stockholders in the Montrose Placer Mining Co. had high hopes of becoming rich. It was estimated that the gravel on Mesa Creek Flats would yield 25 cents to 35 cents per cubic yard of material. The capacity of the operation allowed the company to wash 4,000 to 5,000 cubic yards of gravel per day, and the yield should have amounted to well over a thousand dollars a day.

The placer miners who discovered the fine gold on Mesa Creek Flats had little difficulty recovering gold with their pans; however, the gold was such a fine powder that it washed right through the sluice and remained suspended in the water. It became clear that the entire investment in the flume was lost. Col. Turner became so disheartened over the complete failure of the project that he went to Chicago, rented a room, and shot himself through the head.

The flume was soon abandoned. Ranchers salvaged as much lumber as they could to build houses, sheds, and barns. The rotting remains of the fabulous San Miguel flume still cling to the sandstone cliffs above the Dolores and San Miguel rivers. The flume can be viewed from Colorado 141 near Uravan.

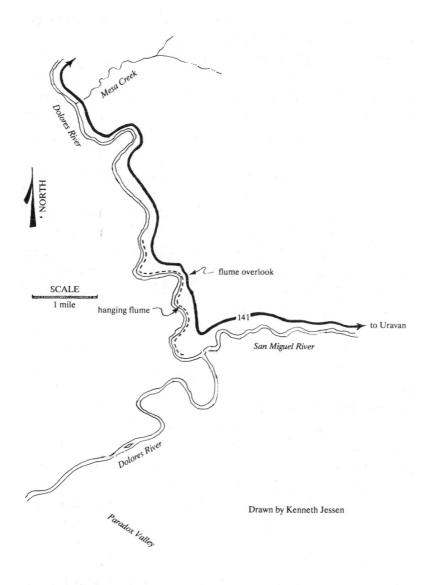

Drawn by Kenneth Jessen

THE TWO-STORY
OUTHOUSE

The thought of a true two-story outhouse, with fully functional facilities on both levels, brings smiles to practically any group. One wonders how such a structure could be designed. Could both levels be used at once or would the lower occupant be in peril from an upper user? The secret of a two-story outhouse is in having the functional portions offset. The advantage of such a facility seems to be in having to dig only one pit and in the ability to service the first and second floors of the main structure. One would think that this might be offset by the added complexity of the design and the possible resistance to use, especially the lower level. The application for two-story outhouses was primarily in multi-story buildings such as hotels and public buildings.

An extensive study of Western evacuation was made by Norman Weis. He traveled to four Canadian Provinces and eleven Western states over a twelve-year period to study the two-story outhouse. In the process, he discovered many such structures. Although Weis did not study Colorado extensively, it is likely that the only still-functioning two-story outhouse in Colorado is located at the back of the Masonic Hall (now known as the Senior Center) in Crested Butte. Heavy snows with drifts in excess of six feet render the lower level inaccessible much of the winter. The upper level, however, is joined to the main building by an elevated, covered walkway. The two levels are offset from each other such that the "business ends" are back to back thus allowing one pit to service both levels.

The second level not only has an access door on its south side from the walkway, but an unused door on the north side leading to nowhere. Nail holes indicate that this second door once served another walkway originating from

Ben Jessen measuring the lower level of the two-story outhouse in Crested Butte. Heavy winter snow renders this level useless much of the year. (photograph by Kenneth Jessen)

another building. At one time, there was a sign over the second-story entrance which read: "Anything over nine pounds must be lowered by rope." To attempt to comply with such a request, especially in urgent situations, seems ludicrous. The sign also requires some interpretation, for example, nine pounds delivered all at once? And how a rope could be used is also a mystery. The sign was probably placed there by some prankster.

The remains of a two-story outhouse are at the back of the Crested Butte City Hall, constructed in 1883. It was an inside type, mounted flush to the back wall of the main building to serve both floors. As Crested Butte moved from a coal mining economy into the ski resort-recreational era, the Marshal's office was expanded around the rear of the building. With part of the office under the second level of the outhouse, it had to be "de-commissioned."

According to Weis, the Elk Mountain House had an incredible outhouse. The structure is now gone, but is memorable for its three stories with walkways from each floor leading to a trio of outhouses with a common pit. The combination of a pit twelve-feet deep and the seat of the upper outhouse sixteen feet above ground level produced a twenty-eight foot drop, providing ample motivation not to fall in!

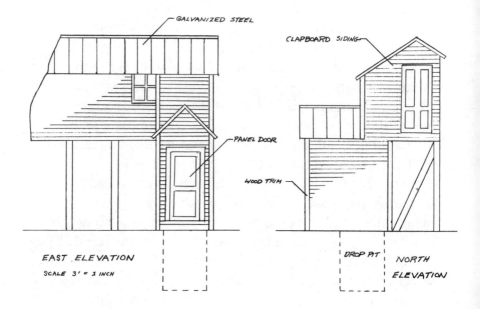

GALVANIZED STEEL

CLAPBOARD SIDING

PANEL DOOR

WOOD TRIM

EAST ELEVATION
SCALE 3' = 1 INCH

DROP PIT

NORTH
ELEVATION

At one time, there was a two-story outhouse attached to the back wall of the Crested Butte City Hall. When the city expanded the Marshal's office, the outhouse was removed from service. (photograph by Kenneth Jessen)

GOLD BRICKS FOR SALE

Doc Baggs was a con man pure and simple, and as his specialty, he only picked on prominent people. Doc knew that once taken, out of sheer embarrassment, such people were unlikely to tell the authorities. Doc Baggs chose his intended victims with the utmost care and always struck for big money. He is credited with originating the gold brick game.

Among Doc's most extraordinary exploits was the sale of two gold bricks to a couple of San Diego mining men. The victims paid Doc $25,000 for their "education" in the gold brick scam. Gold was a magic metal during the Colorado boom years in the late 1800s, and the prospect of owning an entire brick of the precious metal was irresistible to many suckers. The brick was, in reality, nothing more that a common brick covered with a thin layer of gold to allow it to pass a surface assay test.

Doc Baggs also dealt in mining property. He could converse about ore, assay results, mineralization, and other technical matters. He dressed in a miner's uniform to get parties interested in purchasing a share in the underground wealth he located.

Performing these acts often required elaborate staging. His office was rich-looking and contained the finest furniture. An immense safe appeared to be built into one wall. No less than ten square feet, its massive doors were left open so that the victim could peer into its inner depths to view shelving, boxes, and other items while discussing some deal with Doc. Fancy lettering, delicate flowers, and elaborate emblems were added on the safe to impart the feeling of integrity.

The safe was actually a clever painting. In case of an unexpected visit by the police, the safe could be removed

from the wall in seconds. It was a mosaic of numbered,
thin wooden panels each about the size of a cigar box lid.
The painting was on a fabric placed on the panels. The
entire painting could be folded up quickly and carried out
of the building or stored.

As a potential sucker entered the office, Doc would
stand in front of the safe. The rest of the room contained
solid oak counters and the traditional railing with a gate.
The glass in the door leading into the room might be
inscribed with "Private" or "Superintendent" or "Manager"
depending on the occasion. The door was constructed so
that it could be moved quickly into a hiding place built into
one of the walls. Sometimes, the con required a row of
clerks sitting on high wooden stools behind a counter. For
this, he would hire fellow con men to work on thick paper
mache ledgers.

After the sucker was separated from his money, Doc
would fold up his safe, tuck it under his arm, and walk out
of the room. Other props were tucked into hiding places,
the doors were slid back into cavities in the walls, and the
"clerks" would follow Doc out into the street.

One of Doc's men was usually assigned to follow the
victim. If the victim headed to the police, Doc's man would
try to head him off and even offer to return part of the
money. The objective was to avoid trouble with the law.

The victim might frantically get the Denver police and
lead them up to where he was sure Doc's office was located.
The victim might even enter without knocking, pushing the
door open only to reveal a room furnished as a woman's
bedroom. At this point, the police might attach another
meaning to the victim's story.

Michael Spangler, a Denver lawman, tried to put an end

to Doc's activities by arresting him on the charge of "bunco steering." Doc was quick to point out to the court that even in a very large dictionary, the term "bunco steering" did not exist and that no such term appeared in Denver's statutes.

Spangler then assigned Emil Auspity to tail Baggs. When Doc entered into one of his convincing routines for the benefit of a potential sucker, Emil interrupted. The deputy warned the victim he was dealing with Doc Baggs, the most notorious confidence man in Denver. Doc was helpless against this type of harassment and began to use a variety of disguises. It became a game for Doc to dress up in different outfits. After completing a scam, Doc might identify himself to the deputy just to torment him. To vary his trick, Doc got one of his cronies to give Emil false tips as to Doc's identity for that day. Many innocent citizens were falsely accused of being the famous con artist, much to Doc's delight.

Prior to leaving Denver for good, Doc Baggs sold a gold brick to H. M. Smith of Leadville for $20,000. Smith was a banker and took the bait handed him by Baggs. Doc claimed that the gold brick was purchased from a poor Mexican living in a shack. One of Doc's men played the role of the Mexican who claimed the brick was part of the loot taken in a train robbery. Smith had the brick analyzed two years later, and the fraud was exposed.

A HIGH PRICE TO PAY FOR HAY

On August 4, 1890, eight men sat in a cabin socializing. The cabin was located on the Muddy River, about forty miles northeast of the town of Paonia. Of the eight, five were from Kansas and newcomers to the area. The other three men, including Ed Harbinson, were partners in a small cattle ranch.

The group of Kansas men were in the process of clearing rocks, brush, and logs from a twenty-acre mountain park about three miles from the cabin. They planned to cut the lush hay and put it up to feed their stock through the winter.

There was a knock at the cabin door. Ed Harbinson opened the door, and there stood an Irishman named Thomas Welch. The Irishman was prospecting for placer gold and had constructed a cabin about three miles northeast of the mountain park where the Kansas men worked. He remarked to Harbinson, "It looks like you was making preparation to cut hay on my meadow."

Harbinson replied to Welch, "Now listen here, Tom, that park is government land, and we have just as much right to that wild hay as you have."

To that, the now belligerent Welch warned, "If you cut hay on that meadow it will be over my dead body." Welch turned and left abruptly without another word.

Harbinson explained to the others in the cabin that because Welch had cut hay in the park for his burros during the last two or three years, he thought the place belonged to him. No one took the matter seriously, and the men thought that the worst outcome might be a lively fist fight.

The following afternoon around two o'clock, the hay crew was ready to start for the meadow. Harbinson decided to accompany the Kansas men to witness what might turn out to be a good boxing bout with Welch. He also brought along his .45-caliber rifle just in case. Charles Major drove the mowing machine with Harbinson on the seat next to him. The other four Kansas men rode behind.

As they approached the park, no one was in sight. They could see the tall grass swaying in the breeze, and every-thing appeared peaceful. One of the men suggested to Harbinson to relax and put down his rifle. To that, Harbinson replied, "It's funny. From the way he talked last evening, I sure thought he meant business."

The wagon rattled across the grassy meadow, and each man began to feel a little uncomfortable. One of the men shouted to the others, "Take a look at that old log over there about forty feet. I don't remember seein' them rocks chucked around it when we was here yesterday."

All eyes turned toward the log in the northwest corner of the field. The spaces around and under the log were plugged with rocks. Just as the men finished speaking, the muzzle of a rifle appeared over the log. A shot rang out, and a bullet smashed into the mower ricocheting into the air with a whine. The men dove for cover.

Three of the Kansas men on horseback were blasted out of their saddles in a rapid succession of shots. The fourth man hid in the grass as his riderless horse stampeded from the meadow.

Ed Harbinson and the driver jumped from the wagon at the first shot. The driver held the reins and kept down behind one of the wheels. Harbinson crawled into a small depression, keeping low to the ground. More bullets smashed into the mowing machine and struck the wagon wheels.

Harbinson could see that all the gunfire came from the

log. He raised his rifle and returned fire. One round
hit the rocks under the log, and then a hat appeared above
the log. Harbinson fired at the hat band, and the gunfire
from the log stopped suddenly. A voice called out from the
trees along the edge of the meadow, "Take your dead and
get the hell out of here."

Harbinson and the others made a hasty retreat. Thomas Welch and half a dozen armed men came out of the
trees to discover Welch's sixteen-year-old son lying dead
with a bullet through the head. Later, a piece of the dead
boy's skull, with some of his red hair attached, was found
behind the log.

Charges were filed against Welch and his gang. All
were eventually captured and brought before a grand jury.
Thomas Welch and two of the men were indicted, while the
others were released since they didn't participate in the
actual shooting. It was determined that a bullet from
Harbinson's gun killed Welch's son. Harbinson was cleared
of any charges because he acted in self-defense. After a
lengthy trial, Welch and his associates were acquitted in
April, 1891. The facts of the case showed that the boy did
all the shooting. It was a high price to pay for hay.

SPITE FENCES

Ed Stoiber was a wealthy mining engineer and part owner of the Silver Lake Mine high above Silverton. Ed constructed a beautiful home his wife named "Waldheim" at Silver Lake.

Helen was a fearless woman. She often rode in an open ore bucket high over Silver Lake to visit her husband at the mine. She helped him by managing the boarding house. A large woman with a weather-beaten complexion, Mrs. Stoiber was called "Captain Jack" or "Jack Pants" by the miners because of her domineering personality. Her management skills, however, left her husband free to tend to mining and engineering work.

At Waldheim, Helen liked to entertain even though Silver Lake was in a valley high above the town of Silverton. She treated her staff of servants with great kindness, but expected tip-top service in return. At Christmas time, she gave members of her woman's club expensive gifts. If she ended up having a disagreement with any one of them, she demanded the return of the gift.

Superstition played a role in Mrs. Stoiber's life. She was known to delay a luncheon when one out of 14 guests was absent. The luncheon did not begin until a substitute guest was located. At one party, guests were told to put their coats in the master bedroom. Ed Stoiber, unknown to the guests, was in the bed with a cold. When the party was over and the weight of the coats removed, Mr. Stoiber was discovered fast asleep.

Mrs. Stoiber gained fame by the unusual action she took against anyone who really got her upset. Take for example the Hand family in Silverton. They did something that offended Helen, and she reacted by purchasing the lot next to their home. On Sunday morning, when no legal action could be taken, a crew appeared on the lot and put up a large ugly barn.

The Hands sold their home to the Molliques. This family also offended Mrs. Stoiber, and she built a high fence on the lot line on the other side of the Mollique home. The Molliques counterattacked by adding a second story to their home. An ordinance prevented Helen from increasing the height of the fence, so she plastered it with old posters.

Mrs. James operated a boarding house in Silverton for the workers at the North Star mine on Sultan Mountain above town. When she saw the men leaving the mine, she started getting dinner ready. In some way Mrs. James offended Mrs. Stoiber. The result was a nine-foot fence opposite the James home that blocked their view of the mine. Helen commented, "If that doesn't fix her, I'll put pigs in there!"

The Stoibers sold their Silver Lake property for $1.3 million to the Guggenheims. In 1906, Mr. Stoiber was killed in an automobile accident in Paris, leaving behind an estate valued at two million dollars. Mrs. Stoiber accompanied her husband's body back to Denver in a private railroad car, and Ed Stoiber was buried in the Fairmont Cemetery in Denver.

*High above Silverton at Silver Lake was this beautiful
home owned by the Stoibers. Helen Stoiber named her home
"Waldheim."* (from *Pioneers of the San Juan Country*)

LORD OGILVY

Captain The Honorable Lyulph Gilchrist Stanley Ogilvy, D.S.O. was born in London, 1861, to the Eighth Earl of Airlie. His father brought him to Colorado in 1889, at which time the Earl purchased the 3,500 acre SLW Ranch in the northeastern part of the state. The ranch was turned over to the twenty-eight-year-old Lyulph to manage.

Ogilvy found the American West a place of freedom, far different from the formalities imposed on him at home. He was well educated, but at the same time, possessed a certain earthy quality usually not associated with an aristocratic background. Ogilvy stood straight and tall at six-foot-two, but had a sense of mischief. In the words of author Bill Hosokawa, "Legends clustered around Ogilvy the way barnacles attach themselves to a ship's hull."

The ranch was located in an isolated part of Colorado and Ogilvy needed occasional company. For this reason, he frequented the Windsor Hotel in Denver. Here he developed a group of comrades inclined toward the wholesale consumption of liquid refreshments. One story tells of a meeting with Buffalo Bill Cody at the Windsor. Ogilvy remained at the bar beyond the time of departure of the last train north. To solve his need for transportation, he spotted a steamroller near the hotel and drove it to his ranch near Fort Morgan, a distance of more than eighty miles. As the story goes, the trip took most of the night, and Ogilvy would stop the slow-moving piece of machinery for fuel and water along the way. Most of the bridges were wooden, and due to the ponderous weight of Ogilvy's vehicle, later had to be condemned.

Years after this story appeared, his son Jack set the record straight by saying that it was not a steamroller, but rather a steam tractor of equal size. It was purchased by

Lyulph "Lord" Ogilvy as he looked during his youth. He is pictured in the center with two unidentified companions. (Denver Public Library, negative F23260)

Ogilvy to dig a ditch near Fort Morgan. Jack says his
father drove the noisy machine home at night to keep from
spooking teams. The bridges had to be replaced, but in
Lyulph's mind, they needed rebuilding anyway.

The Windsor Hotel remembered Ogilvy for years to
come. When they failed to awaken him one morning, he
returned with a number of cockerels that were just learning
to crow. He released them at five in the morning and woke
many of the guests. He also drove two ponies, hitched
together, into the hotel lobby.

Many of Ogilvy's escapades involved horses. He owned
and raced horses, rode in the steeple chase, and participated in fox hunts. His prize horse was Trooper who
posted a win at Denver's Overland Park during the late
1880s. After the win, Ogilvy invited his friends to his ranch
to honor Trooper. He meant this literally; when his guests
arrived, there was Trooper standing at the head of the
receiving line! To demonstrate the ability of this fine animal, Ogilvy stacked chairs and couches in the center of the
room and had Trooper hurdle them. Trooper, however,
was not accustomed to being indoors and refused to leave
the house. Ogilvy had to remove a section of one wall to
return Trooper to his stall.

When Lady Maud, Ogilvy's sister, came to visit, she was
met at the depot. Ogilvy used a couple of unbroken two-
year old horses to pull the surrey. When Lady Maud
climbed aboard, the horses bolted into a dead run. During
the whirlwind trip to Ogilvy's ranch, Lady Maud didn't say a
word. Near the ranch, the vehicle careened madly, and one
of the wheels splintered. The surrey almost turned over
and came to rest against a tree. Lady Maud stepped se-
renely down and remarked to her brother, "What a charm-

ing place you have, Lyulph."

Later during her visit, she was traveling by stagecoach in California. She was invited to sit next to the driver on the box. On a steep hill with tight switchbacks, brakes smoking, the driver turned to Lady Maud and said, "Ain't you just a little bit afraid?" To that she replied, "I'm used to driving with my brother."

During his early years, Lyulph Ogilvy was reflecting with one of his friends on the brevity of life. They were standing along Larimer Street in Denver as a funeral procession went by. Still recovering from the effects of an excessive amount of liquor the night before, they bet on which one of them would be the principal in such an event. To win the bet, Ogilvy paid an undertaker $1,000 to arrange for the most spectacular funeral Denver had ever seen. A brass band, mourners, and a parade were part of the deal. Besides, the interior of the padded coffin looked quite comfortable, and Ogilvy felt a strong need to lie down.

At 20th Street and Larimer in midafternoon, the parade was assembled. Everything went well until the wagon hit a rut at 16th Street and jarred the coffin. The "corpse" howled at the driver, "Take it easy!"

The driver apparently was not let in on the true nature of this prank. He let out a yell and jumped from the wagon. The horses took off at a dead run, and the coffin fell out on the street. Ogilvy pulled himself out of the splintered wreckage. At the Windsor Hotel that evening, there was a party of even greater magnitude than the one the night before.

During his days of running the ranch, Ogilvy had a housekeeper by the name of Mrs. Wilson. To keep her company, she had a cat, but this animal epitomized feline meanness. Ogilvy owned a bull terrier named Cute. The cat would drive Cute away from his food even though the cat was well fed. When Cute was sleeping, the cat would climb on his back and work its claws into the dog's skin.

Ogilvy kindly suggested to Mrs. Wilson that sooner or later, Cute would lose control and take it out on the cat. Mrs. Wilson replied, "Oh no, Mr. Ogilvy, Cute loves that cat." But Mrs. Wilson failed to estimate Cute's tolerance level. Also, Cute knew better than to show any hostility in the presence of Mrs. Wilson. Patience paid off, and Cute caught the cat away from the safety of the house. He tore the cat limb from limb and then shredded its body.

Ogilvy discovered what was left of Mrs. Wilson's cat and gathered up the pieces in a scoop. He buried it far from the house and did not mention the matter to Mrs. Wilson. When the cat failed to show up, Mrs. Wilson was sure it had fallen prey to a coyote.

Eventually, Ogilvy got married and had two children. His wife became ill, and to pay her medical expenses, he was forced to sell his property. He ended up working in Denver for $1.50 a night as a watchman in the railroad yards. Co-owner of the *Denver Post*, Harry Tammen, knew Ogilvy during his younger years. He spotted Ogilvy at the railroad yards and knew of his extensive knowledge of livestock, ranching, and farming. Tammen hired Ogilvy on the spot as his farm and livestock writer. At the age of forty-eight, Ogilvy was given his own desk at the *Post* and, in turn, gave the newspaper a certain air of respectability. Ogilvy held this job until the age of eighty-three.

Tammen said to Ogilvy, "To hell with calling yourself 'Lyulph.' I wouldn't know what it meant in a thousand years.

You're the son of an Earl, ain't you? Well, you're going
to work for me, and you're going to be 'Lord Ogilvy' to me
whether you like it or not." And so Lyulph was known as
Lord Ogilvy from then on.

Lord Ogilvy used to explain to his co-workers that he
was Scotch and that his clansmen fought among themselves
mostly for exercise and for the sheer joy of living.
Whenever the British would invade from the south, the clan
would stop fighting one another and lick the British.
Afterwards, the Ogilvy clan would resume their own
internal warfare.

It was the custom of the clan to travel lightly in the field.
They took rations of just oatmeal and slept wherever the
day's battle ended. One of his relatives had a son of about
eighteen. At the time, they were engaged in a major battle
with the British. At the close of the day, the senior Ogilvy
was making the rounds in camp to see how his son had
fared during his first conflict. He came upon the boy sound
asleep on the ground with his head resting on a cold rock.
Infuriated, the father kicked the rock from under the boy's
head and remarked, "Let it never be said that a son of mine
was reared in the lap of luxury!"

Lord Ogilvy died at the age of eighty-five in a Boulder
nursing home. He served in the Spanish-American War,
The Boer War (where he was awarded the Distinguished
Service Order) and in World War I.

Lord Ogilvy during his later years working for the Denver Post *as their farm and livestock writer.* (Denver Public Library, negative F11068)

ATTEMPT TO REFORM BRECKENRIDGE

The Methodist Church in Breckenridge was erected by Father Dyer in 1880, and was of a simple design, lacking a belfry. In 1890, during the tenure of Rev. Florida F. Passmore, a beautiful bell was purchased. A belfry was added to the simple 24-foot by 48-foot structure. The bell could be heard through the thin mountain air to call the faithful to services.

Florida's background was not in the ministry. When he first arrived in Colorado he worked as a miner near Alma. Rev. J. R. Shannon, a Methodist presiding elder, met Passmore and was deeply impressed with the spiritual quality of the man. Rev. Shannon encouraged Passmore to enter the ministry. In 1889, after an apprenticeship and training, 45-year-old Passmore was appointed to the Breckenridge Methodist Church.

Passmore immediately moved in as a crusader seeking to change mankind's shortcomings and focused his attention on the miners. He provoked scorn and opposition from many residents in the process. A good example was when a saloon law went into effect in Colorado on April 7, 1891. The law was bitterly opposed by many Breckenridge residents because it demanded that all saloons close at midnight on Saturday and all day Sunday. This was just the type of law Rev. Passmore needed to "improve humanity." He visited all the town's saloons required to comply with the new law. Any time an officer of the law was lax in the enforcement of the saloon law, Passmore got their bond forfeited.

The *Summit County Journal*, August 1, 1891 came out to strongly protest Passmore's crusade in an editorial written by editor Jonathan C. Fincher:

Last Sunday was the Sunday of Sundays; all the saloons in town were closed and their usual habituates were compelled to loaf around the streets. Miners, in from the hills, stood upon the sidewalks looking wistfully to the right or left for some retreat from a condition of misery. To make matters worse, the day was damp and dull. The working of law here was such as to show the sheer nonsense of such legislation for a camp in the midst of the mountains. The law was conceived in the brain of a fanatic, enacted by a body of imbeciles, signed by a doughface, and in a camp like Breckenridge would be enforced only by an impractical enthusiast.

Monday last, a mournful cuss brought in twenty-four stanzas of alleged poetry of which the following six lines are a fair sample:

On the twenty-sixth day of July, year ninety-one,
The drinking community of this town was undone.

On complaint of the parson, by order of the Judge,
All thirsty old toppers were deprived of their budge,

Was denied of the bum, the boss, and the hard-working man.

The editor of the *Journal* poured forth more venom by pointing out how the saloon closure law infringed on an individual's rights and that saloon patrons were not causing any of the town's problems. He also pointed out that the law originated in Denver which was, "...weighed down with cathedrals, churches, chapels and colleges, and crowded with night prowlers, policemen, preachers, priests, and professors..." The editor also pointed out to his readers that the bell called all men and a lot of its cost was paid for by saloon owners and gamblers.

Retaliation against Rev. Passmore was inevitable, and it came on Monday night, August 17, 1891 when the bell and belfry were dynamited. Fragments of the bell were sent in all directions. The culprit was not caught.

This incident galled Rev. Passmore to the point where he dug up an old law passed in 1866 called the Gambling Law. This law had been enforced only in a haphazard way over the years, but now Passmore demanded its strict compliance. All gambling, the primary source of entertainment in Breckenridge, came to a halt. The sheriff of Summit County, F. F. Brown, appealed to Passmore to use reason. He placed the burden on the minister by saying he did more to disturb the peace than all the saloons and gamblers in town combined.

It was difficult for Rev. Passmore to persuade even the courts to assume the right attitude in matters of enforcement. In one incident, Passmore swore out a complaint against a saloon owner for remaining open on Sunday. On February 6, 1892, Judge Eastland directed an undersheriff to read the complaint before the court. The Reverend addressed the court, presenting his side of the case. After a great deal of charges and countercharges, Passmore pointed out that the saloonkeepers were violating the law that stated they were not to open on Sunday. He then shook the American flag until the eagle at the top of the pole appeared to scream. Even after Passmore presented irrefutable evidence, the case was decided in favor of the saloonkeeper!

A new, heavier church bell was ordered and arrived in October, 1891. During the Methodist conference, the church reappointed Rev. Passmore to Breckenridge even though he was not wanted by most of the town's people. His reappointment was celebrated by hanging the Reverend in effigy, and a note was presented to him to leave town. Passmore, however, did not scare easily and remained until a new pastor was selected the following year.

After his departure from Breckenridge, Passmore continued his sermons against drinking and gambling. Finally, in 1896, the Methodists tired of him, and he was expelled from the ministry for anarchy and insubordination. After an attempt to start his own church, Passmore faded into history.

The Father Dyer Methodist Church in Breckenridge was constructed in 1880 and was where Rev. Florida F. Passmore preached. On the night of August 17, 1891, the bell and belfry were dynamited in protest of Passmore's stand on a saloon closure law. (Western History Department, Denver Public Library, negative F28978)

151

THE HEALER

Francis Schlatter was a man with a gentle, child-like simplicity, yet he was powerfully built. This bearded man with long, black hair claimed to be a humble cobbler by trade. In a certain way, he resembled one of the imaginative paintings of Christ.

In the spring of 1895, he appeared in New Mexico looking like a bronze-skinned tramp, but with a self-proclaimed ability to heal. Great numbers of people flocked to him just to be touched by his magic hands in hopes that they might be cured. Most came away claiming Schlatter had ended a prolonged illness or restored full function after a crippling disease. Some Coloradoans made the long journey south to Schlatter's retreat near Santa Fe to be healed. Eventually, he was persuaded to come to Denver and use his unique power. He arrived in the Queen City in September, 1896.

Francis Schlatter was the guest of ex-Alderman E. L. Fox. Schlatter began ministering daily to the multitudes of people who arrived to be healed. They came to Fox's home by the thousands, standing in long lines, waiting to pass by Schlatter to receive his blessing and the gentle pressure of his hand. People also came from the surrounding states. The sick, the maimed, the deaf, the blind, and many others were his subjects. Schlatter made no distinction between age, sex, or station in life. He refused money or favors and accepted only Mr. Fox's hospitality.

As time passed, the daily visitors grew in number until Schlatter was no longer able to touch all that arrived during the course of a day. People began to form a line in the street as early as 3 a.m. and wait until he appeared around 8 a.m. As the chill of winter approached, the multitudes came equipped to camp and to sleep on the ground if necessary. During Schlatter's stay, it was estimated that 60,000 or more came to be healed or simply to see this strange man. Thousands claimed to have benefited from his touch. No one questioned the secret of his mysterious power; they accepted him as a healer with God-given power. Many became so devoted that to doubt his power was a sin in their eyes.

Schlatter was offered large sums of money to go to other cities, but refused. He predicted that he would one day disappear and after a time, return again. On the morning of November 14, about two months after he arrived, Mr. Fox opened the door to Schlatter's room and it was empty. The healer was gone. All of his possessions, except 20,000 unopened letters, were also missing. Fox found a note from Schlatter saying "the Father" had commanded him to leave.

For many days, the disappearance of Schlatter was a great matter of curiosity and a source of grief to those who came to be healed. News arrived that Schlatter was seen riding a white horse into the remote mountains of New Mexico. Other sightings also were made of Schlatter on a horse riding across sandy deserts.

In May, 1897, Schlatter's skeleton, saddle, bridle, staff, and possessions were discovered in a desolate spot in New Mexico. The unofficial verdict was that he died of starvation.

Thousands of people stood in long lines near the home of E. L. Fox in Denver to be healed by Francis Schlatter during the fall of 1896. (Western History Department, Denver Public Library, negative F24078)

The Healer

Francis Schlatter
COPYRIGHTED
NOV. 1-95.

Francis Schlatter seemed to have some unique power to heal people. It is estimated that 60,000 or more came to see this man during his two month-stay in Denver. (Western History Department, Denver Public Library, negative F17543)

In this photograph of Francis Schlatter, his child-like appearance is evident. (Western History Department, Denver Public Library, negative F7591)

DOOMED MONSTERS

Colorado was known as "The Silver State" as its mines continually increased production through the 1880s and into the early 1890s. Prosperity, however, was dependent on the artificial market for silver and gold created by the U.S. Government in minting coins of these precious metals. Various laws were enacted, including the Sherman Act of 1890, to sustain silver production. This act provided for a larger monthly coinage of silver than was the case previously. In 1893, the Sherman Act was repealed and immediately created a depression in the western states known as "The Panic of 1893." Nearly all of Colorado's silver mines closed, and after the panic, only the richer mines were able to reopen. This panic was a turning point for Colorado, and it marked the end of an era.

Naturally, the presidential campaign of 1896 was debated, in part, over the silver issue. The Republicans generally opposed the government's further purchase of silver. Most of the Democrats favored its purchase in a ratio of 16 ounces of silver to one ounce of gold. William J. Bryan was the Democratic candidate for president while the Republicans selected William McKinley.

Coloradoans were vitally interested in seeing the return of the boom era and the reopening of its silver mines. To that end, a stunt to raise money for the Democratic campaign was staged. It consisted of a head-on collision between two locomotives in an arena near the Union Pacific railroad yards not too far from the Grant smelter in Denver. This idea was not new, and successful collisions had taken place in other states. The collision was to occur promptly at 4 o'clock on the afternoon of September 30, 1896.

A pair of small narrow gauge locomotives was purchased from the Union Pacific Railroad. They had a 2-6-0 wheel arrangement and were numbered 153 and 154. The engines were in service a dozen years and were virtually identical. One saw service on the Denver, South Park & Pacific and the other on the Colorado Central.

About ten acres were enclosed with a high fence made of canvas. Through this circular enclosure, a narrow gauge track was laid on dirt about 1,500 feet in length. An additional 300 yards of track were laid outside the fence on each side of the enclosure. The area was designed to accommodate up to 100,000 people. Promoters expected a crowd of at least 60,000 to show and hoped $2,000 or more would be raised by the event.

It was suggested that one locomotive be named "McKinley" and the other "Bryan." The problem with this strategy was that the wrong engine might get the worst of the collision. One of the engines was named "Mark Hanna," after the chairman of the Republican National Committee. The other was named "Bill McKinley." No matter which engine was destroyed, it represented a Republican.

The organizers went one step further than simply naming the engines. Dummies were made to ride in the cabs representing Hanna and McKinley. A dummy of President Grover Cleveland was placed on the pilot of the "Mark Hanna" and a dummy of another Republican sat on the pilot of the "Bill McKinley." The engines were painted red and decorated with bunting and flags. After the decorating was complete, the engines were put on display at Denver's Union Station.

The planned collision velocity was 60 miles per hour. The closest seating to the point of impact was 400 feet. The front of the boilers on both locomotives were drilled

Union Pacific locomotive No. 154 became the "Bill Mc-Kinley," and No. 153 became the "Mark Hanna." These names came from political figures within the Republican Party. These politicians were against the U.S. Government's return to purchasing silver. (Western History Department, Denver Public Library, negative F14011 and F14012)

through and steam pipes attached. The steam pipes projected about three feet in front of each engine, much like a lance. They were designed to break off upon impact to allow steam to escape and prevent a boiler explosion.

During the day of September 30th, the two locomotives with their two-car trains were run up and down the track inside the enclosure. The people arrived in the afternoon to witness the collision. They came by street car, by train, on bicycles, in hacks, buggies, and wagons. Some walked. The sun was warm and the dust awful.

The affair was advertised extensively to take place promptly at 4 o'clock, and at that hour, there were about 6,000 people inside and many more outside the arena. Every vantage point in the vicinity was covered with spectators. This included the telegraph, telephone, and trolley wire poles. Human occupants clung like mammoth birds perched on the very tops of the poles. Every house in the area had people on the roofs. Lemonade and soda water vendors were abundant, and every tenth person seemed to be armed with a camera.

Inside the arena people stood around and tried to find places where they could see. In the center of the arena facing the track, an area was roped off and filled with boards laid over railroad ties. These were the so-called reserved seats. A number of lunch stands did a thriving trade while the people waited. At 4 o'clock, the two trains showed signs of life and ran forward then back through the grounds. The train movements continued at 15-minute intervals for an entire hour.

As the minutes dragged by the crowd began to grow impatient. Nearly all were on time but were forced to wait in the heat and dust. This caused much grumbling, espe-

William H. Jackson captured the crash between two narrow gauge locomotives in 1896 in an arena just outside Denver. The crash was staged to raise money for Democratic candidates running on a platform that favored the purchase of silver by the U.S. Government. (Western History Department, Denver Public Library, negative F138900)

cially because the majority had to stand. Finally at 5
o'clock, the engineers and firemen climbed onto their
respective locomotives after being given brief instructions.
At around 5:15, the trains backed outside the fence. A man
with a flag took his place on a chair in the center of the
track at the supposed point of impact. The flagman waved
his flag. The "Bill McKinley" responded with two short
whistles, and the "Mark Hanna" responded from the other
side. The flagman waved his flag again, and again the
whistles responded. Once more the signal was given with
the flag. The "Bill McKinley" started to puff and the "Mark
Hanna" did likewise. The engineer on the "Bill McKinley"
pulled the throttle wide open, tied down the whistle, and he
and his fireman jumped off on opposite sides of the cab as
the engine began to move. For some unknown reason, the
train of two cars was left behind.

The flagman grabbed his chair and ran away from the
track. The crowd noticed that the "Mark Hanna" was doing
a vast amount of puffing, but was making no headway. The
engineer had pulled the throttle open, but the sudden
application of power caused the wheels to spin on the track
without taking hold. Many of the spectators stood within
ten feet of the south gate where the "Mark Hanna" was to
enter. In the meantime, the "Bill McKinley" came thunder-
ing and puffing with its whistle shrieking into the arena at
an ever-increasing speed. It was now clear that something
had gone wrong and that the collision would not take place
where it was planned. Soon, the "Bill McKinley" sped past
the center of the arena and a warning was given to the
people near the south gate to get away quickly. Men,
women, and children raced back to safety.

The crash took place about thirty feet inside the south

gate. The "Mark Hanna" had just begun to pick up speed. The impact was followed by a roar of escaping steam. The estimated speed was only 30 miles per hour, half the speed the promoters advertised. The engines struck squarely and rebounded about ten feet from the point of impact. The air was filled with fragments of wood and iron, then steam and smoke hid everything. After all the steam had escaped, men and boys climbed all over the wrecked locomotives and picked out small scraps as mementos of the event. The spectacle was over. The crowd slowly began its way out of the dusty arena back to Denver.

The "Bill McKinley" got the worst of the wreck with its tender torn loose from its frame. The cab was crushed, and one of the pony trucks was driven under the lead driver. The pony truck from the "Mark Hanna" was torn loose and ended up in front of the other locomotive. The "Mark Hanna" had one of its cylinders broken off, and its tender was also torn loose from its frame.

The event did not meet with media approval. The *Rocky Mountain News* reported the next day in its headlines "Fifty Cents for a Fizz" and "A Spectacular Disappointment." The *Denver Evening Post* reported "Badly Fooled Crowd."

The damaged locomotives were taken to the U.P. shops, repaired, and renumbered Colorado & Southern 2 and 3. They served the railroad for several more years and were sold sometime prior to 1902.

The "Bill McKinley," shown on the right, got the worst of the collision with its tender wedged into the cab. (Western History Department, Denver Public Library, negative F40341)

HIGH ALTITUDE
FIREWORKS

Climbing mountains in the summer can be dangerous, but climbing in the winter greatly increases the risk of injury or frostbite. Irrespective of the season or weather conditions, travel by foot above 14,000 feet adds to the risk. Climbing a peak over 14,000 feet every year on New Year's Eve, independent of the weather conditions, possibly takes the cake among mountaineering traditions. But this is just what makes the Ad Am An Club so famous.

The story of the Ad Am An Club began in 1906. As their mother waited patiently, Fred and Edward Morath made their first climb to the summit of Pikes Peak. It was June, and the boys found themselves all alone on the summit of the great mountain. After her ten-hour wait at a picnic table near the cog railway track, her sons returned.

On December 31, 1922, Fred and Edward decided to hike to the top of Pikes Peak once again. They wanted to celebrate the New Year on the 14,110 foot summit, and they carried some fireworks with them for the occasion. They invited three other veteran mountaineers to go along, including Fred W. Barr, who constructed the Barr trail up the east face. These men later became known as the "frozen five."

Their trip began at Manitou Springs early in the morning. Along with their provisions, they also carried two hundred pounds of rockets and other fireworks. About five o'clock that afternoon, the party arrived at the summit. After tunneling through snowdrifts to gain access to the summit house, they built a roaring fire in the potbellied stove. They formed a New Year's "watch party."

At midnight, the men set off their high altitude display in the first fireworks of its kind. Many people saw the bright explosions from Colorado Springs, and the men

One of the Ad Am An Club's founders, Fred Morath, pictured in 1924. (James L. Bates collection)

agreed to do it again the following year. Fred Morath suggested that the party add a new member every year and the term "add-a-man" was coined. It later was converted into the Ad Am An Club name.

The following year, six members of the Ad Am An Club scaled the peak via the cog railway tracks to again form their "watch party." A series of signals were fired beginning at 7 p.m. and every hour thereafter until just before midnight. The lights on Platte Avenue were turned off and on in Colorado Springs to signal the men on the summit.

The fireworks began with three 50,000 candlepower flares, each with a duration of one minute. This was followed by a battery of rockets, two and ten pounds, forty in all. Giant red powder flares, consisting of forty pounds of slow-burning powder, were set off lasting ten minutes. Wired to the highest point on the observation tower were four intense "electric" torches. These were followed by red, green, and white rockets. The rockets were shot north and south to complete the show.

The 1925 climb was almost a disaster. It was 32 degrees below zero, and Fred Barr suffered severe frostbite as did two other members. Only six men reached the summit. Harry Standley, one of the charter members, took a photograph of the summit house encased in ice. The photo was later made famous when it was published on a postcard.

In December, 1932, a silk balloon was brought to the summit as part of a tribute to Roland Amundsen. This famous Norwegian explorer was lost in the Arctic in 1928 and was made an honorary member of the Ad Am An Club. The balloon carried a 500 candlepower magnesium flare. That particular year, the club set off a ton and a half of fireworks.

In 1949, fourteen members started out on December 30 for the summit and were equipped with walkie-talkies. The progress of the climb was broadcast every hour using a radio link in Colorado Springs. At 9 p.m., five fireworks were shot into the sky to honor Zebulon Montgomery Pike.

During World War II, it was very difficult to purchase fireworks because of the shortage of gunpowder. In 1944, only a flare was available to bring in the New Year. On this climb, members used automobiles as far as they could up the toll road, then walked the remaining distance. The following year, a token show was all the club could muster using a few six-inch bombs and some rockets.

Upon reaching the summit house in 1952, the Ad Am An Club members discovered the room where the fireworks were stored was packed solid with drifted snow. A small crack in the building combined with the relentless wind drove the snow through the crack where it was packed solid. When the club members arrived, there was little time left until the 9 p.m. display of bombs to honor Zebulon Pike. Members dug frantically to open a tunnel through the room to the fireworks box. Outside, a 50-mile per hour gale pounded the summit house. The display, however, went off on schedule.

In November, 1957 the club announced that the next display from the summit could very well be the last. The Colorado Springs Chamber of Commerce stopped the funding for the purchase of fireworks for the following year. From his home in San Jose, California, Fred Morath sent a check for $10 to try to save the tradition he had helped start. Funding for fireworks from Pikes Peak was reinstated.

By 1973, the Ad Am An Club consisted of 44 members, and 36 made the ascent via the Barr Trail while the remain-

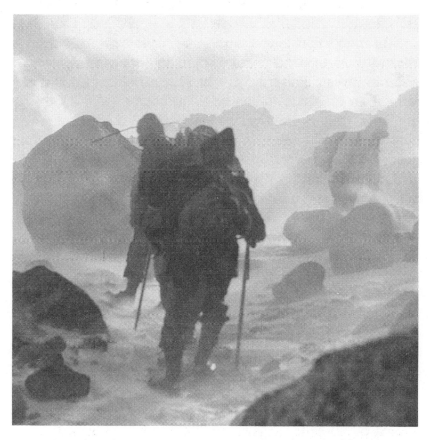

Members struggle against a ground blizzard at 13,000 feet during the 1958 Ad Am An Club climb of Pikes Peak. (James L. Bates collection)

ing members climbed the peak via the automobile road. That New Year's Eve they struggled against 60-mile per hour winds and a wind chill factor of 85 degrees below zero. At 9 p.m., five fireworks were touched off to pay tribute to the original "frozen five." At midnight, cloud cover obscured the display from those in Colorado Springs. Unfortunately, it was the largest display of pyrotechnics set off in 15 years.

The club's 50th anniversary was celebrated in 1972, and Fred Morath (then 79) flew to Colorado Springs from his home in Lisbon, Portugal. His brother Edward (then 78) came from El Cajon, California. The other three members of the original "frozen five" had since passed away. At 9 p.m. on December 31, five rockets were fired in their honor.

On December 13, 1983, the club added its first woman. Sue Graham was an experienced mountaineer. The climb that year consisted of 16 members and 13 guests.

Long live the Ad Am An Club and their unusual tradition, making Colorado and its people quite special.

Ad Am An Club members above timberline on the second day of the 1969 climb of Pikes Peak. (James L. Bates collection)

THE GREAT
HORSE RACE

The *Denver Post* sponsored an endurance horse race in May, 1908. First prize was $500, and the distance was 523 miles beginning at Evanston, Wyoming. The race followed what is now Interstate 80 to Cheyenne, then turned south to its conclusion in Denver. The race was staged to settle the old argument between horse breeders about the durability of the venerable western bronco vs. the eastern thorough-bred.

During the preceding months, the *Denver Post* launched a vigorous advertising campaign to search for entries. Among those who stepped forward were Dode and Ben Wykert of Severance, Colorado. They operated a livery barn and both were good horsemen. They viewed the event as a challenge and purchased a blue roan named Sam from a family west of Ault for $100. The brothers agreed that Dode would ride Sam, and the men began a rigorous training program. The horse was put on a diet of oats with a small amount of hay.

Charles Workman, a resident of Cody, Wyoming, also began training for the endurance race with a horse named Teddy. It was rumored that Teddy was backed by Buffalo Bill Cody and several other wealthy race horse enthusiasts. Workman rode Teddy fifty miles a day and also rode his horse from Cody to Evanston, a distance of about 500 miles. Teddy looked like such a strong contender that a representative from Cody was sent to Denver with $3,000 for betting purposes.

In all, the race attracted twenty-five riders; thirteen were full or part thoroughbred. The remaining horses were western broncos. The largest entry was Rose at 1073 pounds. R. H. Failing of Littleton was the heaviest rider at 223 pounds, atop a 900-pound chestnut named Tom Camp-

bell. Charles Workman weighed only 160 pounds and
was the lightest rider. His horse Teddy weighed 1025
pounds.

The *Denver Post* arranged for a special train to transport
many of the riders and their mounts to Evanston for the
start of the race. The Union Pacific Railroad placed
watering stations for the horses along the route. The most
difficult section was the Red Desert between Rock Springs
and Rawlins. The race rules required horsemen to register,
rest, and feed their horses every fifty miles.

Early in the morning, May 30, 1908, the great horse race
began with a send-off speech by Wyoming Governor Marshall Hadsell, followed by a reading of the rules. Amid
shouts and shots, the riders took off. Teddy went through
three bucking sprees during the early part of the race until
he settled down. Charles Workman then put Teddy into a
fast pace to outdistance the rest of the field. Dode Wykert
and his horse Sam, however, quickly saw how easily they
could stay with the leaders.

The first one hundred miles across the Red Desert was
quite telling on riders and animals alike. Soon the field
narrowed to just fifteen riders. Workman and his horse
Teddy strayed from the course and were forced to back-
track for two hours. They made up the time, and Workman
rode Teddy alone into Rawlins at 1:16 p.m. on June 1.
They were now 243 miles from the start of the race. W. H.
Kern of Colorado City was only five miles behind. Dode
and his horse Sam were ninth into Rawlins and didn't arrive
until the following morning. They placed dead last among
the riders.

In the next leg of the race, Workman and his remarka-
ble horse were first into Laramie. When Dode, riding Sam,

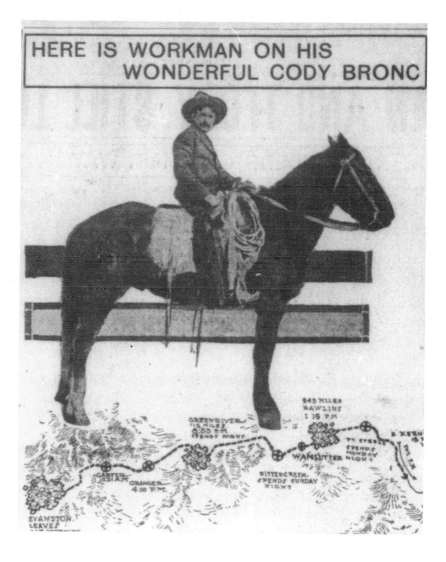

Charles Workman on his horse Teddy is shown in the Denver Post *above a map of the route through Wyoming.* (Colorado Historical Society)

entered Laramie, the other riders were well ahead at
Tie Siding. Over the Sherman Mountains between
Laramie and Cheyenne, Sam showed his real power and
Dode showed his endurance as a rider. Dode and Sam
pulled into the lead and led the way into Cheyenne eleven
minutes ahead of Workman. They were escorted into town
by a welcoming committee of one hundred riders, including
the state's governor.

All the horses were given a thorough checkup in Cheyenne. The field was now down to five, with four of the
remaining horses western broncos. All the riders mutually
agreed to bed down for the night and start out the following
morning at the same time. Workman was given permission
by the judges to rest at the stable of one of his backers. Just
after midnight, Workman violated his agreement and saddled up Teddy. Quietly they slipped out of Cheyenne under
the cover of darkness. One of Workman's backers rode
ahead and left a faint trail of flour along the route south to
Denver.

Fortunately, a couple of newsboys spotted Workman
leaving town and alerted the other riders. Within minutes,
Dode saddled Sam and was off in hot pursuit.

Around two a.m., four of the riders reached Carr, and
Workman realized his scheme had failed. Dode's supporters, however, countered with a trick of their own. As
Workman slept, Dode and Sam quietly moved out of sight
and waited. Dode's supporters got a horse and rider of
about the same size as Dode and Sam. The rider dressed
exactly like Dode. They left Carr at a terrific pace, and
someone shouted to Workman, "Wykert's left! Get the hell
out of here!"

Charles Workman leaped to his feet. What he saw were

a horse and rider he believed were Sam and Dode
leaving a trail of dust across the prairie. He exclaimed as he
rode off, "They won't catch me napping! I'll give them the
race of their lives!"

The gap between the horses closed, and as Workman
brought Teddy alongside the other rider, he shouted,
"Thought you'd fool me, did you?"

A reply came back, "Who in the hell would I be trying to
fool?"

Workman suddenly realized he had been tricked. He
had pushed Teddy hard, and his horse was spent. Dode was
within sight of Workman and could have passed him easily.
Dode, however, showed restraint and saved Sam for the
final push into Denver.

Workman arrived in Ault at about 3:45 a.m. A horse
named Jaybird was in second place. Dode jogged Sam in
about fifteen minutes later. The citizens of Ault built a big
bonfire and greeted the riders as they entered town. Dode
caught up with the two leaders by the time he and Sam
reached Eaton.

Between Eaton and Greeley, Workman's supporters
tried another trick. They used an automobile to stir up a
cloud of dust ahead of Dode. The driver kept the car in the
middle of the road, blocking Dode and Sam. Dode was
prepared, and pulled out a revolver. When he threatened
to shoot the car's occupants, the driver quickly yielded the
right-of-way.

In Greeley, all three horses were examined, and Jaybird
was ordered out of the race by the veterinarian as unfit to
continue. Western broncos Sam and Teddy were now the
only surviving equestrian contestants. Teddy was so weak
that escort horses were held close to each side to support

*Dode Wykert and his horse Sam are pictured in front of
the State Capital Building in Denver after completion of their
523-mile horse race starting at Evanston, Wyoming.*
(Colorado Historical Society, negative F11254)

him. Teddy was given shots to keep him going, and at
Fort Lupton, the horse was fed whiskey and quinine. Dode
knew it was just a matter of time and endurance before
they would win the great race.

A big blow came to Dode near Brighton, when officials
declared the race a draw. Both horses were said to be unfit
to go on with their riders, and the riders were ordered to
walk their horses the rest of the way into Denver. They
were instructed to cross the finish line together. Protests
and accusations were shouted at the officials. After all, a
lot of money was riding on the outcome.

Using an automobile, the horses were led into Denver
along a road lined with thousands of people. As the procession turned on Champa and moved its way toward the
finish line in front of the *Denver Post* building, Dode
mounted Sam and made an attempt to pass the pace car.
As 25,000 spectators watched, Dode faked Sam to the left
of the car, and the driver maneuvered to block their way.
Dode and Sam then shot ahead on the right to cross the
finish line first.

The race had taken seven days, and the horses had
traveled 523 blistering miles. Despite the fact that Dode
and Sam crossed the finish line first, the race was still declared a draw. Because Sam was in far better condition, the
Wykerts received the $300 best condition award. Sam lost
only fifty pounds during the contest versus two hundred
pounds for Teddy. Many gifts, including a $500 silver
trimmed saddle, pairs of boots, and a riding outfit, were
presented to Dode.

Teddy was unable to move for almost three days, while
in contrast, Sam was allowed to graze on the capitol lawn.
Buffalo Bill Cody invited Dode and Sam to join his Wild

West Show on their European tour. Dode modestly declined the offer.

Dode said after the race, "...and I will get backing for $5,000 that I can take this Teddy horse over a six-day race and beat him at the finish. I ain't saying that I can stay with him the first few days. No horse can do that and live. But I can come from behind and get him just as I got him this time."

Since only Western broncos finished the race, there was no question that they were far more durable than the thoroughbred in a long-distance race.

A very tired-looking Charles Workman from Cody, Wyoming, is pictured after the conclusion of the great horse race. (Colorado Historical Society, negative F33072)

PIGG HUNTS BEAR

The legend of Old Mose began in the fall of 1883 when Jacob Radliff traveled forty-five miles from his home in Fairplay to the Black Mountain area to hunt deer and elk. Meat of this type was a staple for the miners, and the game in the Fairplay area had been severely depleted. Miners were willing to pay in gold for fresh meat, and this motivated Radliff and his companions.

On their third day of hunting, the men split up. While crossing a small meadow, Radliff saw the tracks of a very large bear. He was not interested in hunting bear and continued across the meadow. As he reached the timber on the opposite side, a huge bear came out of the underbrush directly toward him. Radliff got off one quick shot before the bear hit him and broke the bones in one ankle. The bear grabbed Radliff and bit both of his legs, snapping the bones like sticks. The bear used his claws to slash open Radliff's face and back. The bear seemed infuriated by Radliff's screams and tossed the man into the air. Finally, the bear tore Radliff's scalp off.

One of Radliff's hunting companions heard the shot and the screams. He ran to help, but when he arrived the bear was gone, and the badly injured Radliff was barely conscious. Horrified, he ran and got Radliff's other companion, and the two men placed the injured man on a litter. They carried him back to camp and put him in a wagon. After the horses were hitched, they traveled as fast as they could down the mountain. The jolting on the rough road brought more agony to Radliff as he continued to lose blood.

It was dark when they reached the nearest ranch owned by a family named Mulock. Radliff's bleeding was so great that blood dripped from the bottom of the wagon box. The

injured man was carefully carried inside where Mrs.
Mulock tried to help him. She also put the poor man's
scalp back in place. A cowboy named Hyssong immediately
rode for eight hours in the dark to the nearest railroad
station on the Denver, South Park & Pacific. Here he
telegraphed for a doctor to come from Fairplay. Around
8:00 a.m., the doctor arrived by special train and began the
long ride back to the Mulock ranch with Hyssong.

In the meantime, Radliff suffered through the night, but
did regain consciousness long enough to tell those around
him about the large bear. When he finished, he looked his
companions in the eye and said, "Boys, don't hunt that
bear." A short time later Jacob Radliff died. Hyssong and
the doctor arrived too late. After a well attended funeral,
Jacob Radliff was buried in the Fairplay cemetery.

News of Radliff's death at the hands of a man-eating
bear became the topic of conversation for months to come.
Brave men (after a few drinks) swore to hunt down and kill
the bear. As winter wore on, the bear was soon forgotten
by all except for one individual.

At the small community of Currant Creek, a Pigg became interested in hunting the bear. This was Wharton
Pigg who knew that the bear was now in hibernation for the
winter of 1883-1884. When spring arrived, Wharton began
hunting in the Black Mountain area. He methodically used
a map to mark the location where ranchers reported seeing
bear tracks or, in some cases, having their cattle
slaughtered. After two years, Wharton concluded that the
big bear had a range of 600 square miles, but for all his
efforts, Wharton never sighted a bear of any kind.

Because the tracks of the big grizzly seemed to mosey
around randomly with no particular route, the bear became

The Denver Post *ran this story about the killing of Old Mose in its Sunday edition on May 15, 1904.* (Kenneth Jessen collection)

known as Old Mose. Ranchers continued to report the
big bear tracks and the loss of cattle. Some even claimed to
have gotten off a shot or two at the animal.

Eventually, Wharton was successful at killing a sow and
her cub. In October, 1894, he received some disturbing
news that Old Mose had been killed on Thirty-five Mile
Mountain by a local rancher who had spent the previous
three days hunting the animal. The bear's weight was
nearly a half ton and its carcass filled a wagon box. This
was very bad news for Wharton who remained depressed
all that winter.

When spring came in 1895, however, Wharton found big
footprints once again near Black Mountain. Old Mose was
alive, and all summer long, Wharton hunted the bear. At
times, the tracks seemed only minutes old as Wharton knew
he was hot on the trail of Old Mose.

Wharton discovered gold near Cripple Creek and
worked his own mine to raise money. He realized, however, that he couldn't mine and hunt Old Mose at the same
time. When he sold his mine in 1896, he was wealthy
enough to hunt Old Mose full time through the forests,
meadows and trails near Black Mountain. Eventually,
Wharton purchased the 56,000 acre Stirrup Ranch on the
east side of Black Mountain. It was filled with game and
was a hunter's paradise. The ranch house was only six miles
from where Jacob Radliff was attacked.

At Fairplay, cattlemen built a substantial trap: a pen
with three-foot walls. On one side, there was a gap in the
wall. A dead cow was placed in the pen, and a bear trap
was concealed at the entrance. Old Mose robbed this pen
three times by reaching over the wall and lifting the heavy
carcass out.

A horse killed by lightning on the Dave Walker ranch was left in a pasture surrounded by a stake fence. Every night, Old Mose went into the pasture for a feast. Each time, however, the bear selected a new route, knocked down the fence, and walked through the break.

Old Mose became a legend in his own time. August Hall was gathering raspberries near the Stirrup Ranch, and after filling his pails, he started back home. In the thickest portion of the bushes, he heard a snort. Not fifty yards away was Old Mose standing on his hind legs.

As stated by Hall, "Suddenly my feet started running. No forethought had propelled them. Never before had I dreamed I was a born sprinter. As if by arrangement, my feet brought me to a leaning spruce. Without slackening my speed until I reached the top, I 'pine-squirreled' up that spruce tree before the thought occurred to look back at the race - which should go down in the history of speed classics. After reaching the pinnacle of my objective, I looked down to find my 'inspiration' at the foot of my tree. He waddled around, attempting to start up the route I had opened through the thick limbs. Then, as if culling me out as dry meat after his feast on berries, he moseyed away leisurely."

"Arriving home, my wife asked, 'What in the world have you done with your clothes?' Then for the first time I found I had little left of the clothing I wore at the time my feet spoke to me. 'I have just run Old Mose four miles,' I told her, not mentioning me being in the lead. My wife had to sit down to do her laughing. I tried to join her, but some-how the laugh wouldn't come."

Wharton knew the bear's range and estimated it took Old Mose around thirty days to make a round trip. Hunting is often cruel, and Wharton purchased a very large steel trap. It was set by a shallow pond in a meadow where Wharton always saw numerous tracks. Old Mose apparently splashed around in the water. Every morning, the trap was watched from a small hill overlooking the pond.

Just when Wharton figured the bear would return, the boy sent to check the trap reported that Old Mose was in the trap. The men at a nearby ranch ran for their guns and climbed the hill. The bear was gone, but his fresh tracks showed he had lost two toes from his left hind foot. The toes were found in the trap and were given to Beulah Beeler Evans who lived on the Beeler Ranch at the base of Black Mountain.

Old Mose was seen many times by a number of people and could now be easily identified by his tracks. He was big enough to kill cattle of any size and was credited with killing three full-grown bulls and a five-year-old Hereford at one ranch. Ranchers claimed that in the fall, just prior to hibernation, Old Mose weighed around 1,500 pounds.

In 1903, a professional hunter named James Anthony moved to Canon City from Boise, Idaho. Anthony killed sixteen bears during the previous year and over forty bears during his life. He was introduced to Wharton and the two men agreed to hunt Old Mose together. Anthony was a slim man with a thin mustache and cold, pale blue eyes. He also had a pack of well-trained dogs.

On their first day out in April, 1904, Anthony and Pigg found the tracks of Old Mose and followed the trail for three days. The dogs finally struck a fresh scent. Old Mose had dined on a dead cow and then had gone into a thicket to rest between meals.

Pigg and Anthony split up; each took some of the dogs.

The dogs that went with Pigg began to bark, but Pigg
was partially deaf and may not have been able to hear
them. Anthony, however, knew his dogs were on the bear's
trail and ran to their location.

As put by Anthony, "I soon came upon the dogs in a
grove of quaking asp <sic> where they surrounded the
biggest bear I ever saw in my life. At first he took no notice
of me and paid but little attention to the dogs while he
walked along, though they were pulling fur every minute. I
fired at about seventy yards. Then I let go three more in
succession, all of which were hits, but none fatal. He stood
on his haunches and looked at me, dropped down and
started for me."

"At about three yards, I took careful aim with my .30-40
Winchester. At this distance, bears generally make a rush
upon a man."

"I got him between the eyes and he fell without a quiver.
It took seven men to get him to the Stirrup Ranch, and we
figured he weighed close to 1,000 pounds."

Anthony headed back to Canon City with his dogs and
wagon. Once he was gone, Wharton Pigg rode back to the
site where "his bear" was killed and blazed the triangle of
trees around the blood-stained ground. He carved on one
tree, "Where Old Mose died" and on another, "Where J.W.
Anthony stood when he fired the fatal shot." Up on the
hillside on a thick aspen tree, Wharton carved "Old Mose's
Last Bed" along with Anthony's name, his name, the name
of the dogs in the pack and the date. Interesting enough,
Wharton Pigg never returned to this spot again nor did he
reveal to his family that he was not the one who had killed
the big grizzly.

A few days after Old Mose was killed, James Anthony

boxed up the hide and the skull and sent it to a taxidermy shop in Colorado Springs. He wanted it made into a rug with the mouth of Old Mose open. The hide was sent by the taxidermy shop to the Arvada Tannery where measurements were made by the editor of *Outdoor Life*. The bear measured ten feet from the tip of the nose to its tail and nine and a half feet from the front of one claw to the claw on the opposite side.

When Anthony left Canon City and moved to Indiana, Old Mose went with him and hung on the wall of his home. Dr. Joseph Grinnell at the University of California, Berkeley wrote Anthony in 1920 asking that he donate the bear to the school. Dr. Grinnell told Anthony that the hide would be well protected and would be available for many years when knowledge of such animals as the grizzly could only be obtained from history.

After Anthony's death, Old Mose was sent to Berkeley. According to James Perkins in his excellent book, *Old Mose*, "If you are ever in Berkeley, California, why not drop in and see the old bear. He's catalogued as MVZ#113385. Tell him Jim Perkins sent you."

It was no surprise that after Old Mose was killed, Wharton Pigg fell into a state of depression. He didn't hold a grudge against James Anthony, and the two men remained friends. After Anthony left the Canon City area in 1907, Wharton tried to build up a good pack of "bear" dogs. He also purchased a new and more powerful rifle. Try as he may, however, he never saw another grizzly bear the rest of his life.

Wharton Pigg eventually lost the Stirrup Ranch and was forced to homestead near Cover Mountain. Here he tried fox ranching, but this too failed. Eventually, he took a job

with the U.S. Biological Service trapping coyotes.
While trapping during the winter of 1930 near Walden, he
was caught in a sudden snowstorm and nearly froze to
death. He got an ear infection and was sent to Denver.
The infection spread, and Wharton Pigg died on March 15
some twenty-six years after Old Mose was shot to death
near Black Mountain.

James Perkins did extensive research into Old Mose
and had one of the bear's teeth dated professionally. The
bear that was killed was in his prime and only ten to twelve
years old. Wharton Pigg had not been hunting the same
bear for twenty years, and this bear could not have killed
Jacob Radliff. The animal that was killed, however, was
the last Black Mountain grizzly.

Grizzly bears have been hunted into extinction within
Colorado, although some believe there are still a few left in
the more remote San Juan Mountains. Bears like Old
Mose simply lived their lives as other bears had done for
tens of thousands of years. Only mankind's desire to hunt
them changed this picture. No longer will the meadows
around Black Mountain feel the weight of a grizzly bear.

THE MAN WITH THE GOLDEN LEG

When Orville Harrington was a boy, a gun explosion during a hunting trip injured his hip and permanently damaged the nerves in his leg. As Harrington grew older, the nerve damage caused him a great deal of pain. He had three toes amputated, then at the age of 42, he was forced to have his foot and the lower portion of his leg removed. Harrington learned to get around on an artificial leg, but it was a turning point in his life.

Orville attended the Colorado School of Mines in Golden and in 1898, graduated with a degree in mining engineering. During his years as a student, he became a class leader and secretary/treasurer of the alumni association. He also managed and edited the school magazine. Harrington was active in a fraternity and maintained good grades.

His injury caused him to limp, and after graduation he was unable to find a job in his field of mining engineering. Hampered by his handicap, he was denied the higher paying engineering jobs. Orville Harrington ended up working the swing shift for $4 a day at the Denver Mint.

Just as Orville finished his shift on a Wednesday evening in February, 1920, Roland Goddard walked over to him. Harrington looked at the stranger and said, "I don't believe I remember you."

"That is unfortunate," replied Goddard, "I am Mr. Goddard of the United States Secret Service. Perhaps you will have an opportunity to know me better in the near future."

At once Orville knew the game was up, breathed a deep sigh, and hung his head in shame. Goddard escorted Orville back into the mint and charged him with embezzlement. The Secret Service spent months trying to figure out how over $80,000 in gold bars was stolen right under their noses. It was the watchful eye of a Secret Service agent that broke the case. Harrington's frequent trips to his back yard with a spade gave him away. After Orville filled a hole in his basement floor with gold bars, he buried them along the sidewalk in his backyard.

Finally, agents planted a piece of gold valued at $1,400 near Harrington's work station just before his shift began. Sometime during the evening, the gold vanished, and when Harrington was searched, it turned up in his vest pocket. The guards never suspected Harrington was carrying the heavy bars because of his awkward limp.

Harrington used a secret compartment in his artificial leg to take most of the gold from the mint. The gold was in the form of 7" x 3 1/2" x 1" anodes created during the gold refining process. The heavy bars easily were inserted undetected through a slot in his artificial leg. In all, he took 53 gold bars from the mint.

Ultimately, Orville planned to take the gold to an abandoned mine in the Cripple Creek area, melt it, and combine it with low-grade ore. His next step was to sell the "ore" back to the Denver Mint as a concentrate.

Orville Harrington and his wife lived a quiet life in a home they had built. They raised fruit trees, vegetables and flowers on an adjoining lot and had two children. When news of Orville's arrest was given to Mrs. Harrington, she was shocked.

On May 12, 1920, at the age of 43, Orville Harrington pleaded guilty to embezzlement and was sentenced to ten years at the Federal Penitentiary in Leavenworth, Kansas. He was paroled three and a half years later. He returned to work for the City of Denver supervising street paving crews. At the age of 50, Harrington quit his job and left his wife and children. Mrs. Harrington was left penniless and had to rent her home. She was forced to live with her children in the chicken coop in their back yard. Eventually, she decided to turn her children over to an orphanage and work as a governess.

Orville Harrington, the man with the golden leg, died at the home of his sister in New York years later.

CENTRAL CITY'S
SUBMARINE

It is preposterous to believe that Colorado would be the site for the development of a submarine. And even harder to believe is that high in the mountains, far removed from any substantial body of water in either size or depth, that this would be where such a development took place. Never-the-less, on an autumn afternoon in 1898, Rufus T. Owens of Central City launched a submarine into Missouri Lake at an elevation of 8,500 feet.

Submarines began to appear during the Civil War, and during the final two decades of the nineteenth century, a number of submarine designs were proposed by a variety of inventors. This activity may have sparked the interest of Rufus T. Owens, and in 1896, Owens began his attempt to design such a craft. He was an engineer and was known for his design of the water distribution systems for both Central City and Black Hawk. This same year, the U.S. was at war with Spain over the sovereignty of Cuba, which was highlighted by the naval battle of Manila Bay. The U.S. considered submarines to be a potentially effective way of defending its coastline against a potential Spanish invasion.

Rufus named his small undersea craft the *Nautilus* after Jule's Verne's fictitious vessel. He hired a pair of Central City contractors to do the actual construction, but kept the work a secret. Owen's craft, built in a small shed in Central City, was nineteen feet long and five feet tall at its center. It was constructed using a wood frame made of hand-hewn, whipsawed lumber held together by handmade square nails. After completion of the frame, the exterior was covered with irregular-size sheets of iron carefully soldered at the seams to create a seaworthy craft.

On the day of the launch, Owens hired the owner of a local livery company to use a flatbed wagon to haul the

Nautilus to Missouri Lake three miles north of Black Hawk. This was the closest body of water to Central City.

At first, Owens climbed into his craft for its first, untested dive. His friends talked him out of this as being far too dangerous, and he decided, instead, that the craft could be effectively tested using rocks as ballast. The *Nautilus* was pushed out into Missouri Lake for her maiden voyage and immediately sank to the bottom.

Possibly out of embarrassment, Rufus T. Owens left Central City within a year never to be seen again by local residents. Owens showed no interest in retrieving his *Nautilus* from the floor of the small lake. Within two years, the U.S. Navy launched its first successful submarine, the *Holland*.

The existence of the Central City submarine grew more doubtful as time obscured its details. This was combined with the fact that few had actually witnessed the launching, and local newspapers had not recorded the event. During the winter, a surprised ice skater might look down and spot the craft lying on its side a dozen feet below the surface of Missouri Lake.

The Chain O'Mines Company partially drained Missouri Lake during the 1930s, and the *Nautilus* was completely exposed, thus confirming its existence. Its square hatch was stolen by a souvenir hunter. After the lake was refilled, the public soon forgot about the ship.

During World War II, submarine warfare was in the spotlight and interest in the Central City submarine was renewed. One of the few witnesses to the construction of the *Nautilus*, Fred DeMandel, decided to locate and retrieve Owen's ship. As the end of 1943 approached, DeMandel got permission to search the lake by sawing

Lifted from the bottom of Missouri Lake near Central City in 1944, the Nautilus *is raised to the surface. It had been sitting on the bottom of this lake since it was launched in 1898. The* Rocky Mountain News *jokingly termed this the longest dive in history.* (Colorado Historical Society)

holes in the ice in the general area where the ship was believed to rest. On January 11, 1944, after sawing more than a hundred holes and by using a line with a lead sinker, DeMandel finally found the *Nautilus*. He confirmed his find using a glass-bottomed bucket to peer into the water.

The foreman of a local trucking company was hired to raise the vessel using a winch. A large hole was cut in the ice above the *Nautilus* and a steel tripod was erected over the hole. A chain was run through the tripod to the winch. On January 25, the school in Central City was closed along with the courthouse and many businesses to witness the raising of the *Nautilus*. By the time the submarine was hoisted to the surface, 300 spectators were on hand, and the band from the Central City High School played, "Columbia, the Gem of the Ocean."

After the craft dried out, it was put on public display at DeMandel's Central Gold Mine and Museum. It was eventually sold and placed in yet another museum. William C. Russell, Jr., publisher of the *Central City Register-Call* purchased the craft and placed it in a warehouse where it rests today.

Rufus T. Owens built his submarine in secrecy leaving many unanswered questions. The Navy was searching for a practical design at the time, but did Rufus intend to submit his design? When the submarine was raised, no propulsion system or steering mechanism could be found. The ballast weighed around 1,500 pounds, somewhat excessive for a first dive. Maybe the entire project was nothing more than a whim.

Central City's submarine is housed in a Gilpin County warehouse. The craft lacked any propulsion system or steering mechanism leading to speculation that the project was nothing more than a whim on the part of its inventor, Rufus T. Owens. (Colorado Historical Society)

COLORADO'S
APEMAN

Sheriff Richards from Fairplay was acting on complaints from local ranchers in the isolated Black Mountain area of South Park. He was told a crazy man was shackled like an animal in a lonely cabin on the 1,200 acre Beeler cattle ranch. Richards and three officers were sent to investigate the rumors on August 20, 1928.

When the law officers arrived, Mrs. Beeler was sitting on the porch of the ranch house. Her two dogs went into a barking frenzy as the men approached. The officers spotted the log cabin located near the ranch house. They hurried over to the old structure and cautiously peered in through its small window. In the darkness they could see a human form only by the glistening white of his eyes.

Sheriff Richards realized that the stories of a wild man were true. He pried the padlock off the door, and as the door swung open, the officers stepped into the cabin. The sun hurt the wild man's eyes after a dozen years of living in darkness. His fang-like teeth glittered as Colorado's ape-man, Harry Beeler, blinked at the sun. He stared from beneath shaggy, unkempt eyebrows. His matted beard, reaching his abdomen, covered only part of his naked body. A leather belt around his waist was connected to one of the stout chains, and the other end was attached to the cabin wall. A second chain was attached to a leather band around his left ankle. The other end was also attached to the cabin wall.

Harry Beeler sprang at the strangers with a cry like a dog's bark. The chains on the cabin wall stretched tight and abruptly jerked Beeler off his feet. He got up growling and grinding his teeth at the men. The chains prevented him from moving more than three or four feet. In the cabin was a makeshift bed. The floor was piled deep with human

waste, and the odor was sickening. Insects scurried
about in all directions. A tin can on the floor was used for
food.

The seventy-year-old Mrs. Beeler stood by the cabin
and remarked, "He was so bad I couldn't get near him to
touch him. He hasn't had a bath in twelve years since we
got him back from the insane asylum where they put him
after they removed him from the penitentiary. We got him
out through Governor Carlson. I promised to take good
care of him. I did the best I could." She continued her
story of how Harry didn't even recognize his father. He was
so wild that he had to be watched every minute. The only
practical thing left for the family was to chain Harry to the
wall in the old cabin. Sheriff Richards, upon seeing the
tragedy etched on the old woman's face, nodded kindly.

The sheriff and his deputies rushed Harry Beeler from
three sides. The insane man fought like a wild animal.
Finally, the officers were able to handcuff Beeler, and they
threw a blanket over him.

"He hasn't had a stitch of clothes on him for twelve
years," Mrs. Beeler related to the officers, "But every night I
went out after he went to sleep and threw a blanket over
him. Harry is a good boy, Sheriff, and I love him. Harry
was a fine looking boy. Any mother would have loved him
then in the old days. But who but a mother could love him
now as he is today? I don't want them to take him away
from me. It would be better if we were both dead. But I
don't want Harry to die."

Harry and his aging mother were taken in the sheriff's
car to Fairplay. It was the first time in years Mrs. Beeler
had been in an automobile. They put Harry in a cell, and
Mrs. Beeler was given a room in the New Fairplay Hotel.

The August 22, 1928, front page of the Denver Post *shows Mrs. Joseph Beeler and her insane son, Harry, the day he was released from a dozen years of confinement in a cabin on the Beeler Ranch in South Park.* (Denver Public Library, Western History Department, negative F21906)

News of what the media called an "apeman" spread
through Park County. Ranchers and residents came from
all over to see Harry Beeler. The sheriff tried his best to
protect the Beelers from the public and the media. The
next morning, however, people stared through the cell bars
at the poor man, and Harry stared back. Then he dashed at
the bars like a caged lion. The blanket that Sheriff Richards used to cover him was torn to shreds.

Outside on the main street of Fairplay, Mrs. Beeler
protested the way her son was treated. "They won't treat
Harry right in the insane asylum," she told whoever lis-
tened. "They won't feed him what he likes. They won't
cover him at night. They'll just let him die, and while he
might be better off dead, I don't want him to die."

Mrs. Buelah Beeler Evans, Mrs. Beeler's daughter, died
just a week before in a Salida hospital. Her daughter was
known for her books of mounted Colorado wildflowers that
sold all over the United States. Since Mr. Beeler passed
away years before, Buelah's death left Mrs. Beeler alone to
care for her maniac son.

On August 21, 1928, Harry Beeler, age 45, was placed in
the insane asylum in Pueblo after a brief sanity hearing in
Fairplay. First he was bathed, shaved, and clothed. He was
then put in a bed in a private room for observation.

Mrs. Beeler lamented, "I'm alone now. I'm going back
to the ranch to die. I won't live long and neither will
Harry."

The tragic story of Harry Beeler began in 1914 when he
was arrested for stealing and butchering a steer belonging
to a Canon City rancher. After bond was posted, Beeler
disappeared. Harry was eventually located in Buffalo, New
York, through letters he had written home. After Harry

was returned to Colorado, he stood trial. The sheriff told reporters he believed Harry Beeler was innocent and was framed by local ranchers.

Harry, nevertheless, was found guilty and sentenced to a term of two to five years in the penitentiary. After serving a year, Beeler went insane. In 1916, his parents obtained Harry's release to their custody, and this was the last time Harry Beeler was seen for a dozen years. In 1918, Harry's father, Joseph Beeler, died in a South Park cattle war leaving Harry's care up to Mrs. Beeler and her daughter.

After Harry's return to the insane asylum in 1928, Mrs. Beeler moved to Pueblo to be close to her son. On May 3, 1934, accompanied by a hospital guard, Harry was escorted to his mother's room in a Pueblo hospital. No light of reason could be seen in his eyes as he looked at the pitiful figure of his mother lying on her death bed. Drawing his head close to her lips, she whispered all her love to him, closed her eyes, and passed away.

Harry Beeler died at the age of 60 in 1943 in the insane asylum, bringing to a close the tragic story of Colorado's apeman.

Mrs. Joseph Beeler kept her insane son chained to the wall of a cabin for a dozen years before he was rescued by local authorities. (Denver Public Library, Western History Department, negative F21905)

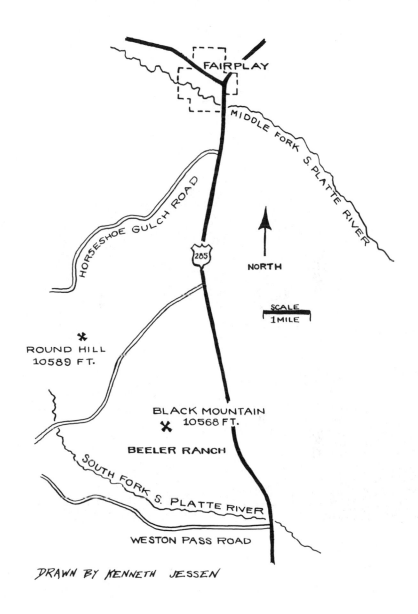

FAIRPLAY

MIDDLE FORK S. PLATTE RIVER

HORSESHOE GULCH ROAD

285

NORTH

SCALE
1 MILE

✸
ROUND HILL
10589 FT.

BLACK MOUNTAIN
✖ 10568 FT.

BEELER RANCH

SOUTH FORK S. PLATTE RIVER

WESTON PASS ROAD

DRAWN BY KENNETH JESSEN

PRUNES

Halfway up Fairplay's main street stands a curious monument made of dull, gray cement adorned with ore samples from many of the mines in the Fairplay-Alma area. Etched in the cement is the following expression of respect to one particular burro called Prunes. It reads, "Prunes - a burro - 1867 - 1930. Fairplay, Alma - All Mines In This District." Expressed in this simple inscription is the heart-felt praise to this shaggy little servant of Colorado. Ripley in his "Ripley's Believe-It-Or-Not" syndicated cartoon made Prunes and his monument famous. Prunes was also featured in 1943 on the radio version of Death Valley Days.

The last mine where Prunes worked was at the Hock Hocking mine in Mosquito Gulch. Prunes became the miners' pet, shuffling back and forth with ore cars in the dark, damp passages. Superintendent Harry Radford maintained that Prunes was his top jackass. When Prunes became too old, his owner Rupe Sherwood freed the jack of his collar and traces, then retired him to roam in the sunlight at will.

When Rupe was twelve, he ran away from home, and after a trip in a covered wagon, ended up hunting with Buffalo Bill. After wandering around the West, Rupe settled in the Alma-Fairplay mining district. For almost five decades, Rupe owned Prunes and boasted that Prunes worked every mine of any consequence in the district at one time or another.

After Rupe "pensioned" his faithful jack, the animal spent its final years making the rounds of Alma's back doors to beg for food. Flapjacks fried in sowbelly grease made old Prunes hee-haw with delight. Residents eagerly gave the old jack food. As the animal approached his 60's, his health began to fail. An examination of his mouth

*On Fairplay's main street stands this unique monument to
a Colorado burro named Prunes. The monument is made of
dull, gray cement adorned with ore samples from the mines in
the Fairplay-Alma area. Behind the monument are the ashes
of Prunes' last owner, Rupe Sherwood, buried there at his
request.* (photograph by Kenneth Jessen)

revealed that Prunes was losing his teeth along with his
ability to eat.

A blizzard struck Alma in 1930, and the snow drifted
deep. The temperature plunged below zero, and Prunes
took refuge in an old shed. During the blizzard, the door
blew shut, and a snowdrift prevented the old burro from
pushing the door open. Residents noticed that the burro
was not making his usual rounds. After searching, they
found Prunes half starved in the shed, weak in the legs, and
unable to walk. He was showered with food and affection,
but did not recover from his exposure to the blizzard.

The miners met in May of 1930 in Alma to decide what
to do about the suffering animal. It was a difficult decision,
and the miners elected to put an end to the suffering of
their little long-eared friend. Prunes was shot as some of
the old-timers, including Rupe, wept. His little gray carcass
was discarded in a local garbage dump.

A Fairplay cafe owner, with the help of other willing
admirers, dug a grave on Fairplay's main street, and here
they deposited the remains of Prunes. Over the grave, the
miners in the area erected the unique cement monument
studded with ore samples from the mines Prunes had
worked. Never before had an animal been so honored by a
Colorado mining town.

Columnist Arthur Brisbane wrote this about Prunes:

An old donkey that worked in Colorado mines so long
that few could remember when he started is dead at
last. He worked until he could not work any more, or
even eat. They shot him. Now he is to be honored with
a memorial, built of ore samples from all the mines in
which he worked. A touching picture, it will be appreci-

ated by many a two-legged worker, including white-
collar men...they are less fortunate than the old mine
burro. Nobody builds a monument to them and nobody
shoots them when they can no longer earn a living.
They are turned adrift.

Rupe Sherwood composed a long poem titled "Me and
Prunes" which begins:

> So poor old Prunes had cashed in.
>   too bad, still in a way,
> I'm glad the old boy's eased off
>   and calling it a day.
> I'm going to miss him scandilous!
>   The world won't seem the same -
> Not having him a-standin' here
>   hee-hawing in the game.

A year later on August 23, 1931 at the age of 82, Rupe
Sherwood died in the Fairplay hospital. On his deathbed,
he realized he was on his last trail. He asked to be cre-
mated and have his ashes buried behind the monument
under which the bones of his faithful burro were buried.
The funeral was attended by about 500 people. A bronze
plaque was added to the top of the monument.

Back at the Hock Hocking Mine, superintendent Harry
Radford instructed his trammer, John Billingsley, to round
up a replacement for old Prunes. The superintendent
didn't care where Billingsley found his burro or how he
trained the animal.

The new jack Billingsley found was a lady which he
named Maudie. The two got along well, but the jack was

difficult to get moving while in her collar and traces. To solve this motivational problem, Billingsley pulled out his plug of Beechnut. Few people knew that a jackass would chew tobacco when given the chance. The burro raised her nose a bit, nuzzled it, and bit off a piece. After that, it was Beechnut for Maudie or no muck was trammed out of the mine. It cost Billingsley a lot of plugs, but was worth the expense.

After a while, Billingsley moved to another mine. One day his old superintendent, Radford, met him near the mine and said, "Billingsley, ye got a right to quit and get another job, but ye ain't got no right to pack away yer secret trammin' tricks. Tell me how in hell ye ever got that bloody damned jack back into that mine?"

Billingsley's response was simple, "It's Beechnut, Harry. Not Horseshoe nor Star, but Beechnut - remember that."

At that, Harry Radford exclaimed, "The hell, and to think Prunes done it all these years without a chaw."

There are a lot of funny stories about burros. For example, a newcomer to the mining regions came across a burro packing a wheelbarrow upside down on its back. The wheel and handles were in the air and the box partially hid the body of the animal. The newcomer asked the owner, "My good man, can you tell me why the little donkey is tied to the wheelbarrow in that odd fashion?"

The owner thought this was a stupid question that deserved a dumb reply, "I shore can, stranger. This here jackax has been acquired by old Walapai Huggins fer a house pet at the Bully Boy mine and bein' as the animule is too dellycat to walk all the way over them rough trails, the old man wheels him up hill and at the summit jes' naturally turns him over on the other side so as the jackax can stand up on its feet. Yessir, it does come hard on old Walapai but its mighty restin' fer the jackax."

A burro's stubbornness and obedience to its master is legendary and is illustrated in the story of a burro named Tom. An old prospector was riding Tom up in the hills, and the animal's rocking motion caused the old man to fall asleep. Suddenly, the animal stepped off into a canyon about 900 feet deep. This woke the old man, and he saw the bottom coming up fast as they fell through the air. He knew they would be killed instantly. Tom liked the old man and would do anything he asked. The old man waited, and when they had fallen to within three feet of the bottom, he yelled, "Whoa, Tom!"

The burro stopped immediately, the old man hopped off onto the canyon floor, and helped lower Tom the rest of the way.

The most important aspect of a burro, at least in the view of mining men, is its load capacity. Exaggerated claims were often made as to how much weight these small animals could carry. The *Colorado Miner* in Georgetown decided to settle this matter once and for all.

It was reported that twenty-one men, women, and children gathered on a June day in 1873 on Georgetown's main street to see how much weight a burro could handle. An eyewitness noted that when 650 pounds were put on the burro's back it began to wink vigorously. At the weight of 1,100 pounds the animal began to shed tears. At a full load of one ton, its tail stopped wagging. At 3,200 pounds, the poor animal exploded. The noise was so loud that it knocked over six men and a baby. Town authorities were so frightened that they thought there was a fire and began to ring the fire bell.

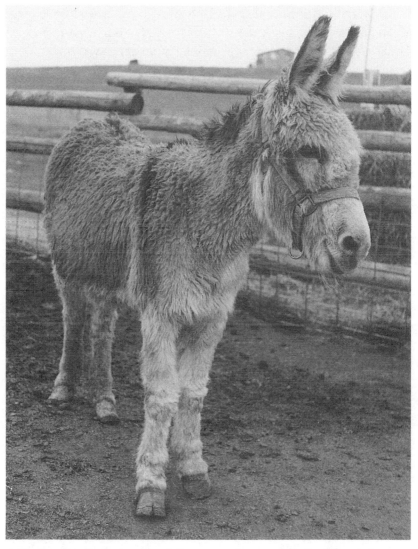

A Colorado burro named Jenny. (photograph by Kenneth Jessen)

LAST PIECE OF
COLORADO

Conflicting territorial claims, changes in sovereignty, and inaccurate maps produced a no-man's-land unclaimed by the United States in the middle of Colorado.

It all began with Christopher Columbus in 1492, followed by claims covering the New World, as it was known at the time, by Spain and Portugal. Exploration by Dominguez, Escalante, and others strengthened Spain's claim on lands west of the Rio Grande River. The French claim of its Louisiana Territory overlapped that of the Spanish. The French explorer LaSalle claimed the entire Mississippi River drainage. The primary area of uncertainty was the border between the western edge of the Louisiana Territory and the eastern edge of the lands included in New Mexico. Since this area was inhabited only by Indians, no real effort was made to resolve the conflict.

In 1762, France ceded its Louisiana Territory to Spain. After nearly four decades, Spain gave the land back to France. England, meanwhile, claimed all land east of the Mississippi River, with the exception of Spanish-held Florida. The American Revolution in 1776 changed the sovereignty of England's claim. In 1803, the French sold the vast Louisiana Territory to the U.S. with its poorly defined boundaries. One thing was certain: the territory included the Mississippi River watershed, to the Continental Divide, and as far south as the future site of Salida.

In 1819, the U.S. signed a treaty with Spain to set the western boundary of the U.S. contingent on the location of the headwaters of the Arkansas River near Leadville. A boundary line was drawn north to meet the latitude of 42 degrees, which was Spain's northern territorial limit. Before it reached this latitude, the line intersected the Continental Divide. This formed a pocket between the Louisiana

Territory, ending at the Continental Divide on its western extreme and Spain's eastern border, ending along a meridian between 106 degrees, 9 minutes to 106 degrees, 25 minutes. The border depended on where the headwaters of the Arkansas River were defined.

Spain's territory, in what is now Colorado, traded hands to Mexico. In 1836, this territory was traded once again to Texas. In 1850, it became part of the U.S., then became part of the State of Deseret, Utah Territory, only to become part of Colorado Territory in 1861. The pocket of land not included under treaty comprised an area roughly 70 miles by 30 miles, forming an irregular oval of about 1,300 square miles from Breckenridge north to Middle Park.

On August 8, 1936, the Breckenridge Women's Club sponsored a unique celebration to officially lay claim to this last piece of land. Colorado Governor Edward C. Johnson unfurled and hoisted the United States flag followed by the Colorado flag. The Governor said, "For that vast territory, he (Napoleon) received 15 million dollars, but this little oval of 'no-man's-land' considered so unimportant that it was overlooked entirely, has produced more than four times the total cost of the fourteen states with which Napoleon so readily parted."

It was sarcastically put by Robert Black, III, in his book *Island in the Rockies*, that "Assuming a permanent division (between the U.S. and Spain), Fraser, Granby, and Hot Sulphur Springs would have found themselves in the United States. Troublesome and Kremmling would have appertained to the Crown of Spain; the formalities of customs and immigration would have been conducted close to the site of Parshall."

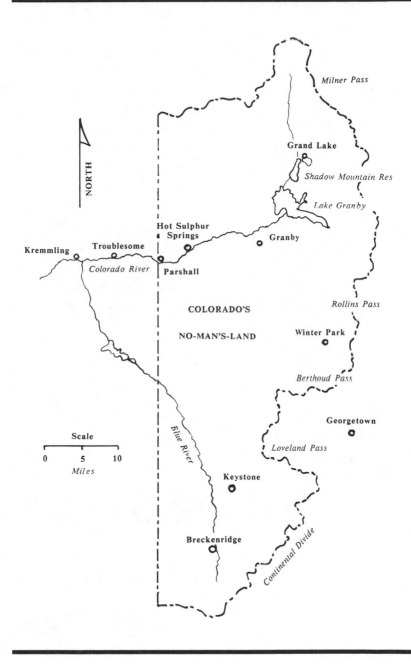

Milner Pass

Grand Lake

Shadow Mountain Res

Lake Granby

Hot Sulphur
Springs

Kremmling

Troublesome

Granby

Colorado River

Parshall

Rollins Pass

COLORADO'S

NO-MAN'S-LAND

Winter Park

Berthoud Pass

Georgetown

Scale

Loveland Pass

0   5   10

Miles

Keystone

Blue River

Breckenridge

Continental Divide

NORTH

MONARCH PASS
ONCE NAMED
VAIL PASS

An article in the November 18, 1939, issue of the *Rocky Mountain News* read, "If You Pass a Certain Pass It Possibly May Come to Pass To Be Vail Pass, Monarch - Agate Pass or Monarch Pass; We Pass!" When Governor Edward Johnson earmarked $1.25 million for the construction of a new highway between Salida and Gunnison in 1937 over Marshall Pass, a controversy developed. Highway engineer Charles D. Vail opposed the route over Marshall Pass until other passes were analyzed. Opposition mounted against Vail's ideas, and the U.S. 50 Highway Association officially condemned any route other than Marshall Pass. The association was headed by local businessmen in Salida and Montrose.

In 1938, Governor Ammons ordered a survey of all possible routes between the two towns. Survey crews worked through the summer and fall, crisscrossing the Continental Divide. From this data, a brand new route following Agate Creek was discovered about two miles south of the old Monarch Pass wagon road. The new route followed the old wagon road up to the town of Monarch where it deviated over the new pass.

The U.S. 50 Highway Association pointed out that Marshall Pass was 440 feet lower than the new Agate Creek route and was easier to keep clear in the winter.

Charles D. Vail prevailed with facts and figures. The estimated cost of the Marshall Pass route was $1.77 million compared to $1.5 million for the new Monarch-Agate Creek route. Also, Marshall Pass required 6,000 degrees of curvature vs. only 4,394 for the new route. The sharpest curves were held to 16 degrees vs. 30 degrees for Marshall Pass. The new route was nearly two miles shorter.

The new highway was constructed and opened for travel

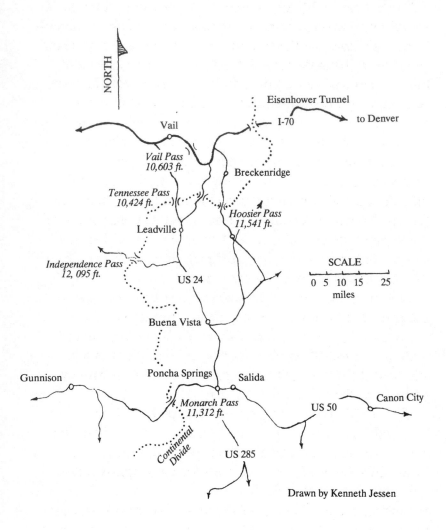

NORTH

Eisenhower Tunnel

I-70 → to Denver

Vail

Vail Pass
10,603 ft.

Breckenridge

Tennessee Pass
10,424 ft.

Hoosier Pass
11,541 ft.

Leadville

Independence Pass
12, 095 ft.

US 24

SCALE

0 5 10 15   25
miles

Buena Vista

Gunnison

Poncha Springs

Salida

Canon City

Monarch Pass
11,312 ft.

US 50

Continental
Divide

US 285

Drawn by Kenneth Jessen

on November 19, 1939. Highway department crews immediately erected signs along the road naming the new route Vail Pass. At the summit, the official state sign read, "Vail Pass, Altitude 11,329 feet," to honor Charles Vail for his years of service to the highway department. The name selected caused both indignation and amusement at the capitol.

In jest, the *Rocky Mountain News* stated, "For the benefit of travelers along U.S. 50 between Salida and Gunnison, it can be stated somewhat officially that the mountain pass between the two communities is either Vail Pass or Monarch-Agate Pass or possibly just plain Monarch Pass. The travelers should not be confused by either road signs or highway maps, state officials said. It is certain that the pass bears one of the three names."

A smear campaign was initiated by local residents. They smeared the Vail Pass signs with black paint.

In an effort to settle the issue for their new Colorado highway maps, H. M. Gousha Co. of Chicago wired Mr. Vail and the governor to determine what official name was to be given to the pass. The governor stated that while some commissioners had decided on the Vail name, the pass should be called Monarch-Agate Pass until the matter was cleared up. "Agate" was dropped from the name, and Monarch Pass won out. The old Vail Pass signs were removed.

In December, 1939, Eagle County Commissioners came to the rescue of Charles D. Vail. The pass between Ten Mile Creek and Gore Creek was known as Low Divide Pass and was traversed by U.S. Highway 6. The commissioners suggested changing the name from Low Divide Pass to Vail Pass. The change was made official and this route was selected for Interstate 70. Ironically, the Vail name is far more prominent now than the name of virtually any other pass in Colorado.

JAPAN BOMBS
COLORADO FARM

When one first learns that Japan bombed a Colorado farm near Fort Collins during World War II, a picture of a heavily loaded bomber flying low over the Rocky Mountains comes to mind. The bombardier squints through the bomb sight as the aircraft makes its run. But this was impossible with World War II technology, Japanese bombers, and the distance involved. Besides, such an event would have been in the history books. The Japanese did in fact bomb Colorado, but not using aircraft. A clever scheme of bomb-carrying balloons was part of an offensive to demoralize U.S. citizens. The Japanese released 9,300 of these weapons between November, 1944 and April, 1945. They counted on the jet stream to carry the balloons over the ocean to the Pacific Northwest where it was hoped the bombs would set fire to our forests.

The balloons were thirty feet in diameter and filled with hydrogen. They carried incendiary and high-explosive bombs, along with a timing device. It required 50 to 60 hours to travel over the Pacific Ocean to North America. To compensate for the slow loss of hydrogen, a barometer triggered the release of sandbags during the course of the flight and kept the balloon within its cruising altitude of thirty to thirty-eight thousand feet. A battery, protected by antifreeze, was used to power the release circuits.

After releasing thirty-two sandbags during the course of the flight, the altitude-control device dropped the load of bombs. This same mechanism also activated slow-burning fuses that set off explosives on both the balloon and altitude-control device. This caused the balloon to self-destruct, producing a blinding flash in the sky as the 19,000 cubic feet of hydrogen ignited. The capacity of this weapon was limited to seventy pounds and was designed to be

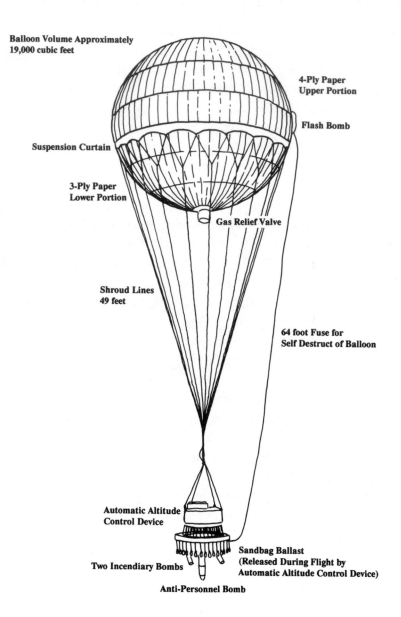

Balloon Volume Approximately
19,000 cubic feet

4-Ply Paper
Upper Portion

Flash Bomb

Suspension Curtain

3-Ply Paper
Lower Portion

Gas Relief Valve

Shroud Lines
49 feet

64 foot Fuse for
Self Destruct of Balloon

Automatic Altitude
Control Device

Two Incendiary Bombs

Sandbag Ballast
(Released During Flight by
Automatic Altitude Control Device)

Anti-Personnel Bomb

unseen until the bombs released and the balloon exploded. The Japanese hoped to psychologically terrorize the American public using this mysterious, silent device that struck randomly without warning.

It took almost two years to develop, and the weapon was designated the "FU-GO." Denied conventional materials due to wartime demand, the Japanese builders turned to the nation's talent for making paper. They used laminated mulberry paper that withstood the cold of the high-altitude flight across the ocean. Balloons were constructed in the homes of civilians, primarily high school girls, as they pasted the necessary four or five layers of paper together.

The Japanese knew of the jet stream, and the November-to-April launch window was selected since the winds were strongest during this period. The one flaw in their thinking was that during these months, the forests in the Pacific Northwest were the least vulnerable to fires. Snow and rain kept the fire danger low.

The launch process depended on good weather and light winds. The balloons were carefully inflated, and it was a dangerous job because of the explosive nature of hydrogen gas. Although they looked under-inflated at launch time, when they reached jet stream altitude the hydrogen expanded to fill the entire balloon.

Of the 9,300 balloons released, the Japanese counted on a thousand making it across the ocean, enough to inflict sufficient damage on the U.S. The Japanese also counted on the media providing detailed coverage of this unusual weapon, and panic spreading across the nation due to its mysterious nature.

As the months passed after the launch, little news came

back to Japan. There was mention in local newspapers of two balloon incidents in Montana and Wyoming in December, 1944. Unknown to the Japanese, coverage was suppressed by a nation-wide effort involving the cooperation of newspaper editors. Having launched over nine thousand balloons, the Japanese concluded that the FU-GO effort had failed and discontinued further production of the weapon.

A design flaw caused the batteries to fail in the cold high altitude because the antifreeze solution was too weak. With no power to release the sandbags, the vast majority of balloons descended into the Pacific. Only a little more than 300 reached North America, hardly enough to be effective.

Most of the surviving balloons landed in the targeted area of the Pacific Northwest, however, none of the bombs started major forest fires. Several landed farther downwind in Montana, the Dakotas, Canada, Wyoming, and Colorado.

There were three confirmed balloon landings in Colorado, plus a number of sightings. The most spectacular incident happened on March 19, 1945, near Timnath. At about 2:00 p.m., a balloon was sighted over Casper, Wyoming, moving to the southeast. By six in the evening the balloon appeared over Fort Collins still traveling southeast. Many residents witnessed the balloon. At 7:12 p.m., a flash came from the weapon followed by a bright ball of fire. Timnath farmer John Swets and his ten-year-old son, Bill, were busy working on some machinery in a shed when they heard the explosion. When they went out they saw a fireball in their newly cultivated field. Sparks flew into the air ten to fifteen feet. A crater measuring about ten inches in diameter and forty-six inches deep was burned into the

ground. Black smoke rose from the crater and drifted
across the field. By 7:30 p.m. a large number of on- lookers
from Fort Collins had arrived. After the danger had
passed, tail fins were recovered from the remains of a
twenty-six pound incendiary bomb. An unexploded incendiary canister was found near the crater.

A neighbor, Frank Richter, found an unexploded bomb
the next day while harrowing his field. It was located a mile
and a half from the Swets farm. The weapon was a ten
pound incendiary. A month later, while driving his tractor,
John Swets hit a cavern left by yet another bomb - a high
explosive type that apparently exploded underground. No
additional bombs were discovered.

The Timnath FU-GO weapon performed the way it was
designed, but it drifted well beyond the intended target
area. Because news of the balloon and explosion was
suppressed, the Japanese never found out about the
Timnath incident during the course of the war.

There were other confirmed balloon-bombs in Colorado near Pagosa Springs, Delta, and Collbran. It is likely
that other balloons landed in Colorado, but were not
observed.

ELIJAH THE MAROONED HORSE

Gordon Warren and Wallace Powell of Gunnison were flying over the high Collegiate Range near Buena Vista during the winter of 1956. They spotted a horse trapped on a ridge between Mt. Harvard and Mt. Yale. Confined to an area about the size of a city block swept clear of snow by high winds, it was obvious to the pilots that the horse would perish unless given some fodder.

Using a Piper Cub, the two Gunnison men began air drops on the 12,800 foot ridge once every few days. Their drops were restricted to times when mountain weather was good. The horse seemed to understand that after the aircraft made an initial pass, it would return to make a drop. Once a bale of hay was delivered, the horse ran over and fed. The mayor of Gunnison, Ben Jorgensen, began paying for the hay and the cost of transportation.

The plight of the marooned horse was brought to the attention of the *Denver Post* by United Airline pilot Ray Schmitt. Schmitt brought in aerial photographs of the animal.

George McWilliams, staff writer for the *Post*, named the horse Elijah after the biblical character who was fed by ravens when lost in the wilderness. Newspapers all over the world published the story of Elijah and the valiant effort of winged Samaritans to keep the animal alive. Children mailed in their nickels and dimes to continue the air drops. TV crews filmed the stranded animal. Centennial Race Track started a fund for Elijah. Many donations were for $12, the cost of a bale of hay. Airline pilots even pointed out the location of the horse to their passengers. Elijah, the rugged, unpampered western horse, soon became a national symbol of his four-legged kind.

From a television news report, Bill and Art Turner of

In April, 1956, an expedition was put together by the Denver Post *to reach Elijah and to check on his condition. Because of deep snowdrifts, Elijah's rescue had to be postponed.* (Denver Public Library, Western History Department, negative F41350)

Buena Vista recognized the horse as one of their pack animals named "Bugs." The Turners recalled that Bugs, a.k.a. Elijah, hated parked cars and women in skirts. He escaped from his mountain pasture the previous fall.

The air drops continued. Then in April, a *Denver Post* expedition, including staff writer George McWilliams, photographer Dean Conger, copy boy Irv Moss, the horse's owners, and ski patrol member Jody Greib, went into the mountains to reach Elijah and check on his condition. It was a long struggle beginning before dawn and lasting until late afternoon, but the Post team did reach Elijah. As they came up on the ridge, the Turners called to their animal, and it walked over to them. They placed a rope halter on him and fed him a bag of oats. Elijah was in fine shape. Deep snowdrifts prevented the team from bringing Elijah down.

Towards the end of May, the Turners climbed through the spring snow and led Elijah down from the mountains. They were forced to shovel a trail through the deep drifts. By the end of the first day, they had made it only part of the way down. They tied Elijah to a picket. When the Turners came back the following morning, Elijah had broken his picket rope and was found a mile back toward the saddle.

The people in Buena Vista came out for a homecoming parade to welcome the hermit horse. Elijah was transported to Denver and became the center of attention at the opening of the quarter horse season at Centennial Race Track. He raced another horse named Goliath and won. Elijah was led to the winner's circle and was presented with a red blanket bearing his name in white letters. Elijah was honored with a parade through downtown Denver, taken to a carnival at the University of Denver, and put on display outside the *Denver Post* building. Elijah was adopted as the official mascot for the Colorado Dude Ranchers Association.

The tale of Elijah was written by Bill Hosokawa, executive news director for the *Denver Post*, and published in the *Reader's Digest*. The story appeared in a dozen languages worldwide.

After all the publicity was over, Elijah was returned to his owners to continue his life as a pack animal for hunters and tourists.

During his last years, Elijah was free to roam in his chosen pastures during the winter months, high above the hustle-bustle of humans. In March, 1971, Bill Turner came across Elijah, crippled and in poor condition. The 27 year-old horse was suffering from a broken leg and could not be moved from his high mountain pasture. Bill Turner did the humane thing and put a bullet into the indomitable old horse. He didn't notify the media at first because he figured Elijah had already had his share of publicity. Elijah's carcass was left in a cluster of rocks among the tall, majestic peaks. This great Colorado horse lives on, however, in the minds of those he touched.

When Elijah, the marooned horse, was led down from a ridge between Mt. Harvard, and Mt. Yale, rescuers were forced to shovel a trench through the snowdrifts. (Denver Public Library, Western History Department, negative F41351)

CRASH INTO MOUNT
SHERMAN

To crash into the summit of a 14,036-foot peak during the winter and survive is amazing. This is just what happened to Orville Rosengren, his wife Lorraine, their son Jack, Chuck Budde, and pilot Jim Williamson. Rosengren operated a car rental agency in Aurora, Illinois and raised quarter horses as a hobby. He planned to show some of his prize horses at the National Western Stock Show on January 13 through 21, 1967. Before the show, however, the Rosengrens and a friend, Chuck Budde, decided on a ski vacation in Aspen. They chartered a plane to take them from Denver to Aspen and took off the morning of January 4. Pilot Jim Williamson originally reserved a supercharged aircraft from Clinton Aviation, but had to accept a normally aspirated Cessna twin engine 310 because of a malfunction in the other aircraft.

Williamson piloted the Cessna up through the clouds to 15,000 feet, but it wasn't long before he encountered a strong downdraft over South Park. The plane lost its lift and fluttered like a leaf toward the ground. After hitting a snowbank, it momentarily bounced back into the air and skidded about forty yards. Chuck Budde was pitched into the aisle of the small aircraft, and Mrs. Rosengren's left arm was broken. No one seemed to be seriously injured.

Williamson found that the radio was still working and called for help on every frequency. Finally, an Ozark Airlines pilot heard the S.O.S. A United Airlines training plane heard only clicks on the radio, and the pilot knew that sound was from an aircraft with its battery about to go dead. Soon, the only sound in the downed aircraft became that of the constant howling wind, and the only thing visible was the blowing snow on a high ridge just below the summit of Mount Sherman. The outside temperature registered 15 below zero.

The aircraft's cabin was intact, but the door was sprung, causing cold air to enter. The luggage was brought in from the wing storage compartment, and the Rosengrens began plugging the gaps in the door with clothing. The rest of the clothing was used around their feet. A bottle of Scotch came in handy during the evening.

When Cluck Budde's shoulder began to hurt, Williamson gave the arm a tug. There was a snap and the pain went away.

The next morning, pilot Bob Greeno and his companion, Elden Larsen, took off from Glenwood Springs in a Public Service Company helicopter. Their job was to patrol the power lines in the more remote areas of Colorado. During the flight, they heard a call over the radio asking if there was a helicopter in the area, and responded. The downed Cessna was spotted by a search plane, and Greeno was able to fly over the ridge right to the site. He landed the helicopter a couple of hundred yards from the aircraft. The helicopter could only hold two passengers, so Larsen stayed behind as the Rosengrens were airlifted to Leadville.

Greeno refueled and headed back toward Mount Sherman. This time, he couldn't land because of extremely high winds. Finally, he found an open area a thousand feet below the first landing site and waited thirty minutes for Williamson, Rosengren's son, and Chuck Budde to descend to him. They all managed to squeeze in and were taken to Leadville just as a snow squall closed the area.

Larsen was now left alone as the weather grew worse. He knew there wasn't any chance for another attempt at landing. He was dressed only in street clothes and decided that his only chance for survival was to head down the mountain. He fell and slid down the slopes of Mount Sherman. In the meantime, a rescue team made its way in a snow cat toward the base of the mountain. Larsen was found and taken back to civilization with injuries and frostbite.

THE TOMATO WARS

What may have precipitated the Tomato Wars was a comment made to Taylor Adams, former owner of the Inn of the Black Wolf at Twin Lakes along Colorado Highway 82. A woman from Dallas looked at the natural beauty of Twin Lakes nestled next to Colorado's highest peak, Mt. Elbert, and said, "This is a pretty area. It's a shame nobody's done anything with it." Taylor knew right then that she had to do something, not about developing the area, but about Texans who constantly try to dominate the economy, the roads, and the resorts.

Many other Coloradoans apparently felt the same way. As many as 500 have shown up at the Tomato Wars to plaster the Texans. Taylor, in fact, had a problem recruiting enough Texans to make the war worthwhile. Non-Texans are even pressed into service to help out by momentarily changing their allegiance. It is not very desirable to be a Texan during the Tomato Wars. Coloradoans historically outnumbered them by as much as ten to one.

To start a war of this sort requires an unusual person with a great deal of imagination. Taylor fits this bill. She is an attractive lady with large brown eyes and short black hair. She probably stands all of 4' 11". Well educated at Harvard, she was a clinical psychologist. She speaks with a slight hint of a Bostonian accent. Somehow, Taylor managed to escape the hum-drum, work-a-day world for a forested piece of property along Lake Creek that she fondly calls Tapawingo. Anyone who loves the out-of-doors would envy the beautiful view from her kitchen window of the stream with the dense forest coming down to the water's edge. Beyond the trees is a rugged mountain rising into the clear Colorado sky.

Taylor has been fascinated with wolves since she was 18

Taylor Adams, well educated at Harvard and a former clinical psychologist, started the Tomato Wars in 1982 near Twin Lakes, Colorado. It began as a protest against the Texans who constantly try to dominate the local economy and grew into an annual event. (photograph by Joel Radtke)

and is a recognized authority on the subject. She lives in a mobile home surrounded by stout wire fences that form separate enclosures. In each enclosure is a pair of wolves. Most of her animals are mature and could easily injure an unsuspecting visitor. She cautions guests not to put their faces close to the wire fences and that only certain animals are safe to pet. Close up, wolves look even more formidable than their photographs. Their wild eyes, large front paws, powerful jaws, and muscular bodies automatically make one cautious when approaching one of the enclosures. After sunset, the wolves join their voices and serenade the stars with their mournful cry. It's a sound not often heard, and one that is not easily forgotten.

The Tomato Wars began in 1982. The contest is held around the middle of September, off season for area resorts. The rules are simple. Soldiers hit above the torso are considered dead and can return to the bar or watch from the sidelines. The battle against the Texans takes place on Saturday, and on Sunday there is a shoot-out to determine the overall winner from among all surviving contestants. Incidentally, the Colorado battle cry is, "Keep Colorado beautiful; put a Texan on a bus."

An army consists of a captain, nine soldiers, and an M.P. There is an entrance fee, and for the 1987 war, this was $375 per army. For this particular war, the winning army was awarded a free night at the Inn of the Black Wolf. The fee covers a T-shirt, a party Saturday night with a live band, plenty of beer, a second party Sunday afternoon, and plenty of tomatoes. Prizes are awarded for the girl with the best "tomatoes," the Texan with the longest horn, and the most imaginative flag. Special prizes are given for the most inventive battle strategy, the best Colorado-Texas joke, and the best costume. Mercenaries are encouraged to participate and are assigned to an army short of people.

Colorado towns, bars, and even companies have sent organized armies to fight the Texans. Creative names such as S.P.O.T. (Society for the Preservation of Overripe Tomatoes), Knights of the Round Tomato, and R.I.P. (Rest in Paste) have been used by various groups over the years. Because it is important to identify members of each army in the field of combat, each Colorado army is given a different colored T-shirt. For ease of identification, the Texans wear either white or yellow.

Some of the best strategy has included a Texan arriving by helicopter, a Coloradoan arriving by parachute, and a peace march held by a dissenting army. In 1984, the inventive Texans moved into battle with a cardboard tank complete with a cannon that squirted tomato juice. The winning strategy one year involved a pretty Texas gal. She began to undress within sight of male Colorado warriors. When the curious Coloradoans advanced, they were ambushed from the trees in a hail of tomatoes. A half dozen casualties resulted before the Coloradoans retreated.

During past wars, simply to survive, the vastly outnumbered Texans have employed elaborate strategies. They have built forts of plastic garbage bags and straw bales and dubbed the forts "the Tomalamo." The Texans located their forts on the south side of Lake Creek, and the flag from the Lone Star State was used to mark its location. The Tomalamo has typically been the scene of the most intense fighting. Incidentally, Lake Creek is temporarily renamed the Rio Grande for the sake of the Tomato Wars.

Taylor "conditions" the ammunition by letting it freeze and thaw for several nights. This has a marked softening

A mock protester and member of S.P.O.T., the Society for the Preservation of Overripe Tomatoes. (photograph by Joel Radtke)

effect. During the more recent years, five tons were used, divided into 265 cases. Each army is typically given three to four cases, and some of the more successful armies are able to steal several more cases.

To review a typical war, a bugle sounds at noon and the throwing begins. As the Coloradoans charge across the "Rio Grande," tomato missiles hit the water all around them much like depth charges. In response to an all-out assault by the Coloradoans, the Texans usually retreat quickly to their fort. They defend their fort by throwing tomatoes at a rapid pace. During some of the battles, the Colorado armies run out of ammunition and are forced back across the Rio Grande. Ultimately, however, the numerically superior Coloradoans surround the Tomalamo, "kill" all the Texans, and bring down the Lone Star flag. This process usually takes about two hours. The hillsides are left running red with tomato juice and, the ground becomes littered with shreds of tomato skins that looked like they came out of a blender.

According to Taylor Adams, the Texans refer to their ammunition as "to-MA-ters" while the more sophisticated Coloradoans often use the term "tom-AH-toes."

During the heat of battle, tomatoes fly in all directions and are split into pieces by tree branches. The soldiers carry their ammunition in plastic grocery sacks strapped to their waists. Many of the participants come dressed in strange outfits and even blacken their faces. Some are in-toxicated, which seems to aid in combat or lessen the agony of defeat. To be drunk, by the way, is technically against the rules. At times, there are close-range encounters between two people faced off only feet apart, throwing tomatoes at one another at a machine gun-like

*Serious fighting at one of the bunkers during the 1989
Tomato Wars near Twin Lakes. Note ammunition boxes.*
(photograph by Joel Radtke)

pace. Bobbing and weaving seems mandatory to stay in the game.

The strategy of some warriors is to simply hide in the woods until the Texans are defeated and the armies are fighting among themselves. These warriors then come out of hiding and wipe out the remaining troops. The survivors from Saturday come to the finals the following day. The first year, the winner was determined by a game of musical chairs where one chair held an overripe tomato on its seat. During the following years, duels were fought at 20 yards. Finalists are not allowed to move their feet, and throwing continues until one of the two combatants gets plastered.

Some years, protestors showed up dressed in outrageous costumes carrying signs with, "Hell No, We Won't Throw" and spouting slogans that tomatoes should be used for bloody marys, picante sauce, barbecue sauce, and other uses. The mock protestors chanted, "Make paste, not waste."

Dressed in a Cuban-style general's outfit, a warrior known only as General Gambola showed up at the 1986 war. He had cartridge belts containing Havana cigars. A female warrior, dressed in a sheep skin outfit with a painted face, held a shield high with the words "Tomato Warrior" painted on it. Maybe the best flag this year was from an army called "Gypsum's Finest" from Eagle, Colorado. It showed an eagle dropping tomato bombs on an armadillo.

The battle zone has varied over the years. For the 1982 and 1983 encounters, the war zone was in a field south of the Inn of the Black Wolf. In 1984 and 1985, the war zone was moved to the upper end of the lake, and from 1986 on, the Tomato Wars were held on Taylor Adam's property along Lake Creek.

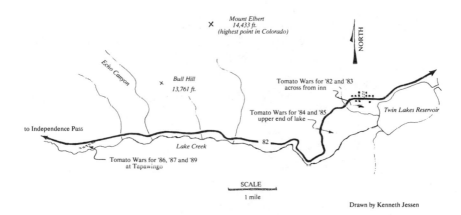

Mount Elbert
14,433 ft.
(highest point in Colorado)

NORTH

Echo Canyon

Bull Hill
13,761 ft.

Tomato Wars for '82 and '83
across from inn

Tomato Wars for '84 and '85
upper end of lake

Twin Lakes Reservoir

to Independence Pass

Lake Creek

82

Tomato Wars for '86, '87 and '89
at Tapawingo

SCALE

1 mile

Drawn by Kenneth Jessen

COLORADO'S
GREATEST BANK
ROBBER

What irritated FBI Agent Charles T. Evans about the so-called "Gentleman Bandit" was what happened on February 13, 1987. The bandit had already struck 40 other banks and just happened to pick one two blocks from his Boulder office. Evans accepted the challenge of putting together the package that ultimately put an end to the "Gentleman Bandit."

In his research, Evans discovered that this bank robber started in Pennsylvania; then suddenly, turned to Colorado. His first bank job was the Silverado Banking Center in Littleton. But every now and then, the robber returned to strike again in Pennsylvania.

The "Gentleman Bandit" was easily identified by the photographs taken by the cameras in the banks. The man they were after was a Tom Selleck look-alike and had a bushy mustache. In fact, a couple of girls in the local FBI office had a great photograph of his behind in jeans and thought he had a great derriere. On his full head of hair, he wore a blue baseball cap. He covered his eyes with sunglasses and carried an athletic bag for his loot. The problem was that he looked like any of two hundred other guys.

This bank robber was not at all a gentleman, but got the name the "Gentleman Bandit" during a Pennsylvania robbery. A little old lady offered him all the money in her purse during one of his holdups. He said that he didn't want her money, only the bank's money. The press got word of this and remarked that this was a gentlemanly thing to do.

According to Evans, this guy was nothing more than a street-wise, smart-ass jerk. There's nothing gentlemanly about a fellow who comes into a bank and points a loaded

9-mm automatic in the face of innocent bank employees.

Evans began his extensive research in Harrisburg, Pennsylvania. He met with about twenty officers and spent three
days brain storming about what this fellow was going to do
next. They ended up with zero.

The task then was divided up between Evans and another agent. Evans took the robberies in the West and the
other agent took those in the East. Slowly they developed a
modus operandi. The robber would leave his own vehicle
somewhere near the bank, but well out of sight. He would
walk to the bank, pull the stickup, and take a car belonging
to a bank employee. He would drive it to his own car with
the money, make the switch, and abandon the other car.

This method was used for many robberies until one day
he took a teller's car only to discover a big German Shep-
herd sitting on the front seat! He switched to leaving the
bank on foot. Next, he began stealing a bicycle for transportation to and from the bank. After each robbery, the
police found the bicycle several blocks away.

The FBI began a program of newspaper ads describing
this robber and invited people to call them. They received
four or five calls a day that went something like, "My
brother-in-law or my ex-boyfriend or my ex-husband is the
guy you are looking for." The FBI spent a lot of time running down leads and found nothing.

By that time, the "Gentleman Bandit" was up to 42
banks and it was the spring of 1987. No progress was made
in solving the case. Agent Evans struck upon the idea of
compiling all the data from all the robberies and then
trying to think like the robber. A questionnaire was developed and filled in for every robbery. The questionnaire

included things like how many tellers there were in the bank, the size of the bank, the type of bank, the time of day, the day of the week, proximity to restaurants, highways, shopping centers, etc. The questionnaire even asked the name of the nearest fast-food chain. The highways were classified into two-lane and four-lane, and the proximity to an exit was noted.

A girl from the Boulder Police Department was brought in to enter all the data into a computer. Using this data base some interesting things surfaced. Every robbery was of a savings and loan with only one exception. The "Gentleman Bandit" also picked on banks in Colorado located only along the Front Range from Fort Collins to Colorado Springs. A similar pattern was repeated in Pennsylvania, but only in a circular pattern. Almost all of the robberies were on Wednesday, Thursday, or Friday and mainly between 1:00 p.m. and 4:00 p.m. There were a couple at 5:00 p.m., several in the morning, and some on Saturday. Of the 44 robberies, 38 fit these times and days of the week. The banks were typically in or near a shopping center with a fast-food chain restaurant nearby. Evans felt that the robber used the restaurant to survey the bank before pulling the job.

Agent Evans then realized that almost no robberies occurred in major towns, but rather that the concentration was in the suburbs. There was only one robbery in Denver, and it was a block and a half inside the city limits near Lakewood. Evans figured it was done by mistake. Why did the bandit pick on the outskirts of major towns? It had to do with the quick response of the police departments in major cities. Denver, for example, had this reputation, and the police didn't mind shooting bank robbers.

The "Gentleman Bandit" only picked on branch banks, mainly Silverado, Empire Savings and First Federal. He avoided Bank Western, possibly because of uniformed security guards.

There were approximately 2,000 branch banks along the Front Range, but eliminating the industrial banks, credit unions, and commercial banks dropped the number. The banks in Denver were also removed from the list, and the number dropped all the way to 200. This was still too many for the FBI to tackle.

During a two-week period, all 200 of these branches were visited. By selecting branch banks in shopping centers, with one or two tellers, no security guard, and a fast food chain nearby, the number was cut to 22. Evans was gratified. He started with potentially 2,000 banks and reduced the number by almost a factor of one hundred.

Next, he called a meeting of the eighteen police departments covering the 22 branch banks. Evans made a presentation complete with slides and overheads. He got commitments from the police departments to place off-duty officers in these branch banks. Because of the manpower involved, they decided to concentrate only on Wednesday, Thursday, and Friday from 1:00 p.m. to 4:00 p.m., the most likely time for the "Gentleman Bandit" to strike.

The next step was to approach the banks themselves. The cost to place an off-duty officer in a bank ran around $300 per branch per week. Because the case might remain unsolved another six months or even a year before the "Gentleman Bandit" was captured, the potential investment was substantial. To make matters worse, some of the banks had several branches in the list of 22. This was a time when savings and loan banks were not doing well. Eventually, all of the bank presidents agreed to pay for the officers.

The branch bank personnel had to be trained. If a teller failed to react correctly, the entire plan could go sour and a teller could get killed. After several months all of the banks had trained personnel. The plan wasn't to shoot the "Gentleman Bandit," but to capture him alive. The tellers were instructed to turn over the money and let him escape. An off-duty officer was to follow on foot and, when outside the bank, make the arrest, hopefully with the help of a uniformed officer.

Evans figured out how long it was between robberies based on the amount of the previous robbery divided by the days to the next robbery. The bandit's take averaged $383 per day. On July 9, 1987, the "Gentleman Bandit" got lucky and struck a bank in Aurora without getting caught, just two weeks after the FBI had it all figured out. At the time there were about eighty officers working at the 22 branch banks from Fort Collins to Colorado Springs. Some were sitting in the parking lots and some were on rooftops with rifles. Because he didn't rob during the designated week, but ten days later, he escaped capture. The police responded immediately and, because the bank was robbed on a Friday afternoon, were reasonably sure it was the "Gentleman Bandit." The officer who arrived on the scene went directly to a nearby apartment complex and immediately found the escape bicycle. Its wheels were practically still turning; the officer missed the bandit by seconds.

October 7, 1987, rolled around and everyone was ready. It was a Wednesday afternoon. At this point, the "Gentleman Bandit" had already hit 49 banks. Inside the Silverado Banking Center in Littleton was off-duty Denver police officer Edwin Morales. He was dressed like a

banker and sat at a desk. The branch manager looked
out of the window and saw a man coming toward the bank
riding a red bicycle. She recognized him immediately with
his full head of hair, sunglasses, baseball cap, and athletic
bag. She said, "That's him."

Morales got into a teller's position, but below the counter. The "Gentleman Bandit" walked through the door and
announced that this was a robbery and asked the tellers to
keep their hands where he could see them. He had his 9-
mm automatic in one hand ready to fire if necessary.
Morales motioned to the bank employees to get down, then
raised up from behind the counter and told the robber to
drop his gun. Morales had his gun ready to fire and pointed
directly at the bandit. The "Gentleman Bandit" brought his
gun up toward the officer, and Morales fired twice. One
round hit the bandit in the chest, he grimaced, doubled up,
and fell to the floor. After three years of investigation, it
was over in seconds. The robber was identified as Melvin
Dellinger.

As Melvin Dellinger was going into surgery, he told the
nurse, "I'm Mel Dellinger, and I robbed 50 banks." Later
he died putting an end to this bizarre chapter in the history
of the West's bank robbers. Melvin Dellinger goes down in
history as the third most active bank robber in the FBI's
files and by far the most successful in Colorado history.

In Dellinger's pocket was a note that explained who he
was and went on to say, "My wife knew nothing about this.
Please tell her I'm sorry. Thanks." On the note was his
phone number, his wife's name, and where his car was
parked that day. It is obvious that he wrote a new note
every time he committed a crime.

Melvin Dellinger entered the Army directly out of high

school and attended warrant officers training in Alabama. He was caught robbing a post PX and was discharged. He then went to college at Pennsylvania State University and eventually received a degree in journalism. In 1975, he robbed a bank in St. Louis and was caught in an attempted robbery in Florida in 1977. For that, he served in a Federal Penitentiary. After four years, he was released. He completed his parole in November of 1982, but began robbing banks again. Dellinger left his native state and moved to Denver in 1984.

Dellinger lived a fairly normal life in Denver and was liked by his neighbors. He went to a local health club to stay in shape. He was friendly, but too lazy to work for a living. Dellinger and Elizabeth Zwinak rented a home on Elm Street in Denver. They weren't married when they started renting, but later Dellinger began to refer to Elizabeth as his wife.

What did he do with his money? He lived modestly. He paid his rent and bought food for himself and his wife. He kept his yard nice and lived a quiet life on South Elm. When he left on a bank-robbing trip, he told his wife he was going on a business trip. His father was in the carpet business, and Melvin supposedly went on the road selling carpet for his dad. Neighbors simply believed he made his living this way. His real expenses, however, were those incurred in gambling - so much so that he was a preferred customer at Caesar's Palace in Las Vegas. He also gambled at the casinos in New Jersey.

The irony of this story is that the same bank he first robbed in Colorado was his last.

Bank camera photographs of Melvin Dellinger, Colorado's greatest bank robber. He was readily identifiable with his full head of hair, a baseball cap, sunglasses, and a 9-mm auto-matic. (photograph courtesy of the FBI)

BIBLIOGRAPHY

JULESBURG: A TOWN ON THE MOVE

Annals of Wyoming, Vol. 7, No. 2, October, 1930, pp. 306, 375.

"Army Whipped - Wagons Burned - Many Killed." *Miner's Register*, Central City, January 1, 1865.

Breihan, Carl W. "Captain Joe Slade, the Big Wolf." *Real West*, Fall, 1974, pp. 45-49, 80.

Collins, Dabney Otis. *The Hanging of Bad Jack Slade*. Denver: Golden Bell Press, 1963.

Darwin, Wayne. "Who Really Condemned Slade to Hang?" *Western Frontier*, May, 1985, pp. 38-43, 58.

Dunning, Harold Marion. *Over Hill and Dale*. Boulder: Johnson Publishing Co., 1956, pp. 576-580.

Eberhart, Perry. *Ghosts of the Colorado Plains*. Athens, Ohio: Swallow Press, 1986, pp.. 215-221.

Gates, Zethyl. *Mariano Medina*. Boulder: Johnson Publishing Co., 1981, pp. 67-68.

Langford, Nathaniel Pitt. *Vigilante Days and Ways*. Montana State University, 1957, pp. 360-376.

Lee, Wayne C. "Julesburg, the Wandering Town." *True West*, March, 1983.

Long, James A. "Strange Truth about Jack Slade." *Golden West*, October, 1974, pp. 8-10, 45.

O'Dell, Roy P. "Did 'Jack' Slade Really Have Four Ears?" *Quarterly of the National Association and Center for Outlaw and Lawman History*, Vol. IX, No. 4, Spring, 1985, pp. 16-17.

Patterson, Richard. "Was 'Jack' Slade an Outlaw?" *Quarterly of the National Association and Center for Outlaw and Lawman History*, Vol. IX, No. 4, Spring, 1985, pp. 14-15.

Shackleford, William Yancy. *Gun-Fighters of the Old West*. Girard, Kansas: Haldeman-Julius Publications, 1943, pp. 11-12.

"The Indians in Force - Our Troops Retreat." *The Leavenworth Times*, January 9, 1865.

"Town Cleaned Out." *Rocky Mountain News*, January 9, 1865.

Twain, Mark. *Roughing It*. Hartford, Conn: American Publishing Company, 1872, pp. 104-119.

Watrous, Ansel. *History of Larimer County*. Fort Collins: Courier Printing & Publishing Co., 1911, pp. 73-75, 75-76, 105-106, 189, 191.

Werner, Fred H. *Heroic Fort Sedgwick and Julesburg*. Greeley: Werner Publications, 1987, pp.. 19-27.

Wilkins, Tivis E. *Colorado Railroads*. Boulder: Pruett Publishing Co., 1974, p. 31 and p. 35.

INDIAN EATER BIG PHIL

Hafen, LeRoy R. "Mountain Men - 'Big Phil', the Cannibal." *Colorado Magazine*, Vol. XIII, March, 1936, No. 2, pp. 53-58.

White, Philip W. "Twelve Colorado Characters." *The 1967 Denver Westerner's Brand Book*, Vol. XXIII, Denver: The Westerners, 1968, pp. 276-277.

Zamonski, Stanley W. and Teddy Keller *The '59er's*. Frederick, Colorado: Platte N Press, 1961, pp. 47-48.

WILLIAM S. WILLIAMS, M.T.

Favour, Alpheus H. *Old Bill Williams - Mountain Man*. Norman: University of Oklahoma Press, 1962 (copyright 1936).

Field, Matthew C. "William S. Williams M.T." *Colorado Magazine*, Vol. XV, No. 2, March, 1938, pp. 73-76.

Hafen, LeRoy R., ed. *Mountain Men and Fur Traders of the Far West*. Lincoln: University of Nebraska Press, 1982, pp. 193-222 (from an article by Frederic E. Voelker, "William Sherley (Old Bill) Williams").

Pomplun, Ray. "Old Bill - He had a Passion for Solitude."
Denver Post, *Empire Magazine*, April 22, 1979, pp. 34-39.

THE DEADLY RAT GAME

Hanchett, Lafayette. *The Old Sheriff and Other True Tales*.
New York: Margent Press, 1937, pp. 25-30.

THE PICKLED SKULL MYSTERY

Bair, Everett. *This will be an Empire*. New York: Pageant
Press, 1959, pp. 31-35.

Brown, Robert L. *Ghost Towns of the Colorado Rockies*.
Caldwell, Idaho: Caxton Printers, 1977, pp. 224-225.

STEEL SPIKE TURNED TO SILVER

Digerness, Helen. "Jesse Summers Randall and Pioneer
Georgetown." *Colorado Magazine*, Vol. XXII, No. 4,
1945, p. 263.

Editorial Notes, *Colorado Magazine*, Vol. XXIV, No. 1,
1947, p. 43.

DUELING MADAMS

"A Free Fight." Denver *Times*. August 25, 1877, p. 2. col. 3.

Bancroft, Caroline. *Six Racy Madams of Colorado*. Boulder:
Johnson Publishing Co., 1965, pp. 32-39.

Miller, Max. *Holladay Street*. New York: Ballantine Books, 1962, pp. 99-104.

Parkhill, Forbes. *The Wildest of the West*. New York: Henry Holt & Co., 1951, pp. 207-286.

"The Denver Park Row." *Rocky Mountain News*, August 25, 1877.

THE LOST LOCOMOTIVE

Interview with Elizabeth Sagstetter, May 29, 1988.

Iron Horse News, February, 1978. (A publication of the Colorado Railroad Museum, Golden, Colorado)

"Kansas Pacific Train Swept Away." Colorado Prospector, Vol. 4, No. 9, p. 1 (from the Denver *Times*, May 22, 1878, May 23, 1878, May 29, 1878 and the *Rocky Mountain News*, June 1, 1878)

Nicholson, N.H. "Memories of the Lost Union Pacific Train." Ohama: Union Pacific Archives, Union Pacific Museum.

Sagstetter, Elizabeth. "The Locomotive That Never Returned." *Denver Post*, *Empire Magazine*, May 21, 1978, pp. 36-39.

Sanford, Albert B. "The Lost Locomotive." *Colorado Magazine*, Vol. XIV, No. 4, July, 1937, pp. 157-158.

BABY TOSSED INTO BLIZZARD

Nossaman, Welch. "Pioneering in the San Juan." *Colorado Magazine*, Vol. XXXIV, No. 4, October, 1957, pp. 300-304.

A COLORADO CACTUS TRAGEDY

Ross, A. R. "Early Colorado Cactus Tragedy." *The Colorado Magazine*, Vol. XXIV, No. 5, September, 1947, pp. 191-194.

COUSIN JACKS

Friggens, Paul. "The Curious 'Cousin Jacks'." *The American West*, Vol. XV, No. 6, (November/December,1978), pp. 4-7, 62, 63.

Friggens, Myriam. *Tales, Trails and Tommy Knockers*. Boulder: Johnson Publishing Co., 1979, pp. 93-94.

Murphy, Michael, "When The Cousin Jacks Came to Central City." *Denver Post, Empire Magazine*, July 5, 1981, pp. 14 - 18.

Thompson, J. T. "Cousin Jack Stories." *Colorado Magazine*, Vol. XXXV, No. 3, July, 1958, pp. 187-192.

A CURE FOR TALLOW MOUTH

Blair, Edward. *Leadville: Colorado's Magic City*. Boulder: Pruett, 1980, p. 62.

Canon City Record, February 16, 1939.

THE GREAT ROCK WALL

Hauck, Cornelius W. "The South Park Line, A Concise
History," *Colorado Rail Annual* No. 12. Golden:
Colorado Railroad Museum, 1974, pp. 150, 151, 190.

Ormes, Robert. *Tracking Ghost Railroads in Colorado*.
Colorado Springs: Century One Press, 1975, p. 70.

Poor, Mac C. *Denver South Park & Pacific*. Denver: Rocky
Mountain Railroad Club, 1976, pp. 232-235.

BOSCO'S BAGGAGE

Crum, Jose Moore. *The Rio Grande Southern Railroad*.
Durango: San Juan History, Inc., 1961, (taken from
"Snakes in the Depot" by John Houk), p. 288.

MASKED MARRIAGE

Ayers, Mary C. "The Bridegroom Wore a Mask." *Pioneers of
the San Juan Country*. Durango: Sarah Platt Decker
Chapter D.A.R., 1952, Vol III, pp. 16-17.

PIE OVEN CREATES TRAFFIC JAM

Sprague, Marshall. *The Great Gates*. Lincoln, Nebraska:
University of Nebraska Press, 1964, pp. 256-258.

COLORADO'S MAGNIFICENT FLYING MACHINES

The Colorado Prospector, Vol. 2, No. 3, March, 1971, pp. 3-4. (from the *Rocky Mountain News*, June 11, 1903, and *Denver Republican*, January 22, 1888)

A DOUBLE-BARRELED THREAT

Burroughs, John Rolfe. *Where the Old West Stayed Young*. New York: Bonanza Books, 1962, pp. 230-231.

THE SAN MIGUEL FLUME

Rockwell, Wilson. *Uncompahgre Country*. Denver: Sage Books, 1965, pp. 160-166.

GOLD BRICKS FOR SALE

Collier, William Ross and Edwin Victor Westrate. *The Reign of Soapy Smith*. New York: Doubleday, 1935, pp. 27-29.

Robertson, Frank G., and Beth Kay Harris. *Soapy Smith*: *King of the Frontier Con Men*. New York: Hastings House, 1961, pp. 31-37.

A HIGH PRICE TO PAY FOR HAY

Rockwell, Wilson. *Sunset Slope*. Denver: Big Mountain Press, 1956, pp. 230-235.

SPITE FENCES

Camp, Mrs. A. M. "Helen Allen-Webster-Stoiber-Rood-
Ellis." *Pioneers of the San Juan*. Durango, Colorado:
D.A.R., 1952, pp. 143-148.

Fast, August. "What I Remember." *Pioneers of the San Juan*.
Durango, Colorado: D.A.R., 1946, p. 154.

LORD OGILVY

Baskett, Floyd. "Mrs. Winston Churchill's Legendary Uncle
Lyulph." *Empire Magazine, Denver Post*, April, 1957, pp.
12-13.

Fowler, Gene. *Timberline*. New York: Garden City
Publishing Co., 1947, pp. 110-114.

Hosokawa, Bill. *Thunder in the Rockies*. New York:
William Morrow & Co., 1976, pp. 85-93.

Ogilvy, J. D. A. "Certain Adventures of L. Ogilvy." *Empire
Magazine, Denver Post*, October 18, 1970, pp. 8-11.

Ogilvy, J. D. A. "As a Horseman He Convinced the
Cowboys." *Denver Post, Empire Magazine*, October 25,
1970, pp. 41-45.

Parkhill, Forbes. *The Wildest of the West*. New York: Henry
Holt and Co., 1951, pp. 124-126.

ATTEMPT TO REFORM BRECKENRIDGE

Fiester, Mark. *Blasted, Beloved, Breckenridge.* Boulder:
Pruett Publishing Co., 1973, pp. 185-194.

THE HEALER

Hall, Frank. *History of the State of Colorado.* Vol. IV.,
Chicago: The Blakely Printing Co. 1895, pp. 458-459.

Magill, Harry B. *Biography of Francis Schlatter the Healer.*
Denver: Schlatter Publishing Co., 1896.

DOOMED MONSTERS

Kindig, Richard, E. J. Haley and M. C. Poor. *Pictorial
Supp.lement to the Denver, South Park & Pacific.*
Denver: Rocky Mountain Railroad Club, 1959, pp. 145-
156.

The above reference includes the following articles:

Denver Evening Post, September 24, 1896

Denver Evening Post, September 25, 1896

Rocky Mountain News, "Bumping of the Engines."
September 25, 1896.

Rocky Mountain News, "Two Doomed Monsters."
September 27, 1896.

Rocky Mountain News, "Will Come Together."
September 30, 1896.

Rocky Mountain News, "Fifty Cents for a Fizz."
October 1, 1896.

Denver Evening Post, "Badly Fooled Crowd."
September 24, 1896.

HIGH ALTITUDE FIREWORKS

"Ad Am An Club Adds a Woman." *Denver Post*, December
13, 1983.

"Ad Am An Club Plans Greeting to 1945 But on Modest
Scale." Colorado Springs *Gazette Telegraph*, November
20, 1944.

"Ad Am An Fireworks Display This Year Could Be Last."
Colorado Springs *Gazette Telegraph*, November 26,
1957.

"Ad Am An Groups May Scale Peak from Two Directions."
Colorado Springs *Gazette Telegraph*, December 29,
1953.

"Building Balloon to Carry Huge Flare from Peak New
Year's." Colorado Springs *Gazette Telegraph*, December
11, 1932.

"Climbers at Barr Cabin for Night." Colorado Springs
Gazette Telegraph, December 31, 1937.

"Cloud Cover Kills Ad Am An Display - Climbers Faced 85 Below Chill Factor" Colorado Springs *Gazette Telegraph*, January 2, 1974.

Dudley, Charles S. "I Remember." Colorado Springs *Gazette Telegraph*, December 5, 1965.

Fetler, John. *The Pikes Peak People*. Caldwell, Idaho: The Caxton Printers, 1966, pp. 260-267.

"History of the Ad-Am-An Club from 1922 to 1965." Denver Public Library clipp.ing file (author unknown).

"Spectacular Greeting to New Year Tomorrow Night by Ad Am An Club." Colorado Springs *Gazette Telegraph*, December 30, 1923.

The First Fifty Years of Ad Am An 1923-1973. Colorado Springs: Ad Am An Club, 1973.

"2 Ad Am An Founders Recall 1906 Climbing 'Thrill'." *Denver Post*, December 12, 1972, p. 25, B 7.

"Walkie-Talkie will Report Progress of Adaman Climb." Colorado Springs *Gazette Telegraph*, December 28, 1947.

THE GREAT HORSE RACE

Black, Winifred. "Man and his Bronco!" *Denver Post*, June 1, 1908, p. 1.

Harvey, Robert Emmet. "Workmen and Teddy still Lead *Post* Race." *Denver Post*, June 2, 1908, p. 1.

Harvey, Robert Emmet. "Workman Got Start of Others." *Denver Post*, June 5, 1908, p. 1.

Kelly, Elizabeth. "Denver *Post* Race Officially Decided." *Denver Post*, June 7, 1908, p. 1.

Krakel, Dean F. "Dode Wykert and the Great Horse Race." *Colorado Magazine*, Vol. XXX, No. 3, July, 1953, pp. 186-193.

Miller, Charles. "Last of the Racers has Passed Rawlins." *Denver Post*, June 3, 1908, p. 2.

"Teddy and Sam Run Dead Heat in Great Race." *Denver Post*, June 6, 1908, p. 1.

Van Loan, C. E. "Workman and his Big Bronc, Teddy, Lead Race into Rawlins Alone." *Denver Post*, June 1, 1908, p. 1.

Van Loan, C. E. "Four Run Abreast in Lead of *Post's* Race," *Denver Post*, June 3, 1908, p. 1.

Walker, George S. "Endurance Race Leaders are within a Day's Ride of the Finish." *Denver Post*, June 4, 1908, p. 1.

PIGG HUNTS BEAR

Bair, Everett. *This Will Be an Empire*. New York: Pageant
  Press, 1959, pp. 252-260.

"Career of 'Old Mose,' a Noted Bear, is Cut Short." *Denver
  Republican*, May 3, 1904, p. 1.

Everett, George G. and Dr. Wendell F. Hutchinson, *Under
  the Angel of Shavano*. Denver: Golden Bell Press, 1963,
  pp. 257 - 261.

Perkins, James E. *Old Mose*. Manitou Springs, Colorado:
  Herodotus Press, 1991.

Queal, Cal. "The Grizzly that Terrorized Colorado." *Denver
  Post, Empire Magazine*, January 28, 1968, p. 3.

Sterling, Janet. "A True Bear Story." *Rocky Mountain
  Empire Magazine*, July 7, 1946.

THE MAN WITH THE GOLDEN LEG

"The Man with the Golden Leg." *The Colorado Prospector*,
  Vol. 3, No. 5, May, 1972, p. 5. (from the *Rocky Mountain
  News*, February 6, 1920).

CENTRAL CITY'S SUBMARINE

Harper, Frank. "Rufus Owens and his Central City
  Submarine." *Colorado Heritage*, Autumn, 1993, pp. 13 -
  18.

COLORADO'S APEMAN

"'Apeman' is Calm in Insane Hospital." *Denver Post*, August 22, 1928, p. 1. col. 8, p. 3. col 1.

"Authorities Scout Tale of Riches Told by Apeman's Kin." *Denver Post*, August 24, 1928, p. 7. col 1.

Bair, Everett. *This Will Be an Empire*. New York: Pageant Press, 1959, pp. 267-281.

Beeler, Mrs. Joseph. "Mother of 'Apeman' Tells Pitiful Story." *Denver Post*, p. 1. col. 7, 8, p. 5, col. 2.

"Blaze Razes Shack that Housed Maniac." *Denver Post*, July 29, 1930.

Brady, Ralph. "Chained 'Apeman' Rescued from Cabin." *Denver Post*, August 21, 1928, p. 1. col. 7, 8. p. 5. col. 1.

"Death of Insane Survivor ends Beeler Cattle King's Tragedy." *Denver Post*, August 5, 1943, p. 8. col 2, 3.

"Fairplay, 'Apeman' suspected of Mystery Killing in 1916." *Denver Post*, August 29, 1928, p. 21. col 1, 2.

Wayne, Frances. "Mother, Loyal throughout Life to Apeman Son, Dies in Pueblo." *Denver Post*, May 4, 1934, p. 3. col 7, 8.

"Worry over Arrest Wrecked Beeler's Mind, Says Ex-Sheriff." *Denver Post*, August 22, 1928, p. 3, col. 7, 8.

PRUNES

Brookshier, Frank. *The Burro*. Norman, Oklahoma:
University of Oklahoma Press, 1974, pp. 257-259.

Bair, Everett. *This Will Be an Empire*. New York: Pageant
Press, 1959, pp. 174-179.

Davidson, Levette J. "Rocky Mountain Burro Tales." *1950
Brand Book*. Denver: The Westerners, Vol. VI,
pp. 193-203.

"Burro Bursts." *Colorado Prospector*, Vol. 13, No. 12, p. 7
(from *The Colorado Miner*, June 6, 1873).

LAST PIECE OF COLORADO

Black, Robert C. III. *Island in the Rockies*. Granby,
Colorado: Grand County Pioneer Society, 1969, pp. 19-
20.

"Colorado's 'Forgotten Empire' is Officially Annexed by
U.S." Denver *Post*, August 9, 1936, sec. 5, p. 7.

Ives, Ronald. "The Colorado 'No-Man's Land'." *Colorado
Magazine*, Vo. XXIV, No. 2, March, 1947,, pp. 66-73.

MONARCH PASS ONCE NAMED VAIL PASS

"Eagle County Demands Pass Be Name Vail." *Rocky
Mountain News*, December 7, 1939.

"Governor's Order Ends Strange Political Feud Between Highway Engineer and Road Association." Durango *Herald Democrat*, December 5, 1939.

"Grins and Groans Greet 'Vail Pass' Highway Signs." *Denver Post*, October, 31, 1939.

"If You Pass a Certain Pass It Possibly May Come to Pass to be Vail Pass, Monarch-Agate Pass or Monarch Pass; We Pass!" *Rocky Mountain News*, November 18, 1939, p. 6.

"Monarch Pass Road Showdown at Hand." Denver *Post*, July 17, 1938, p. 1, sec. 1.

"New Mountain Pass over Continental Divide is Thrown Open to Travel." Pueblo *Star Journal*, November 19, 1939.

"Row Over Name Still Rages as Pass is Opened." Denver *Post*, November 18, 1939.

"'Vail Pass' Proposed for Monarch Pass." *Rocky Mountain News*, August 30, 1939.

JAPAN BOMBS COLORADO FARM

Getz, Robert. "The Bombing of Timnath." *Choice* (*Coloradoan*), September 7, 1986.

"Japs Bombed Timnath Area." Fort Collins *Coloradoan*, August 15, 1945.

Schuessler, Raymond. "Attack on America by Balloon." *Modern Maturity*, February-March, 1985, p. 4.

Unsworth, Micheal E. "Floating Vengeance: The World War II Japanese Balloon Attack on Colorado." *Colorado Heritage*, Autumn, 1993, pp. 22 - 35.

ELIJAH THE MAROONED HORSE

Fenwick, Red. "Elijah Finished His Last Winter." Denver *Post*, September 19, 1971, p. 49.

Hosokawa, Bill. *Thunder in the Rockies*. N.Y.: William Morrow & Co., 1976, pp. 335-337.

McWillaims, George. "Rescue Teams Head for Elijah; Humane Society in Warning." *Denver Post*, April 12, 1956, p. 2. c. 3.

McWillaims, George. "Post Climbers Find Elijah Fat and Sassy." *Denver Post*, April 13, 1956, p. 2.

McWillaims, George. "Shaggy Elijah Rescued from Mountain Retreat." Denver *Post*, May 24, 1956.

McWillaims, George. "Tale of 'Elijah' Snowbound Horse Circles Globe in Dozen Languages." *Denver Post*, February 7, 1956.

"Of Hay in Special Airlift." *Denver Post*, April 8, 1956.

"*Post* Team Finds Elijah Safe." *Denver Post*, April 13, 1956.

Queal, Cal. "All the World Loves a Horse - Even 'Swaps'."
   Denver Post, May 14, 1956.

"Storied Mountain Horse Being Led from Lofty Ridge."
   Denver Post, May 23, 1956.

CRASH INTO MOUNT SHERMAN

Reckler, Joanne. "5 Saved from Plane Near 1000-ft. Cliff."
   Rocky Mountain News, January 6, 1967, p. 5.

Marvel, William. "Snowy Crash Survivors Treasure Life."
   Rocky Mountain News, January 6, 1967, pp. 5-6.

Reckler, Joanne. "Copter Pilot Modestly Tells of Rescue."
   Rocky Mountain News, January 6, 1967, p. 24.

THE TOMATO WARS

Carrier, Jim. "Seeing Red." *Denver Post*, September 27,
   1987, p. 6B.

Frazier, Deborah. "Splat! State Ripe with Pride After
   Smearing Texas in Tomato War." *Rocky Mountain
   News*, September 27, 1987, p. 34.

Interview with Taylor Adams on Sept. 3, 1988 at her home
   near Twin Lakes, Colorado.

Interview with John Slater on Sept. 3, 1988 at the Nordic
   Inn, Twin Lakes, Colorado.

Jameson, Betsy. "Colorado Tomatoes Puree Texas
 Invaders." *Network*, December, 1984, pp. 16-19.

Knox, Don. "5th Tomato War Makes 'em See Red." *Rocky
 Mountain News*, September 14, 1986, p. 40.

McCoy, Joan "Twin Lake Inn is Rustic, Friendly." *Rocky
 Mountain News*, March 6, 1983, p. 50N.

McCarthy, Larry. "Tomato Wars." *Philip Morris Magazine*,
 Spring, 1988, 34-37.

Noriyuki, Duane. "Tomato War Party Swings at Twin
 Lakes." *Rocky Mountain News*, September 30, 1984, p. 8.

"Twin Lakes Gears Up for Annual Colorado vs. Texas
 Tomato War." Loveland *Reporter-Herald*, September
 13/14, 1986.

COLORADO'S GREATEST BANK ROBBER

Talk given by Agent Charles T. Evans at the Greeley Public
 Library, May 20, 1988.

"Bandit a Gentleman and a Scholar, Too." *Denver Post*,
 December 8, 1987, p. 1.

"Officer Shoots 'Gentleman Bandit' Suspect." *Rocky
 Mountain News*, October 8, 1987, p. 1.

"Gunshot Ends Career of Suspected 'Bandit' Where He
 Began Spree." *Rocky Mountain News*, October 9, 1987,
 p. 1.

INDEX

Browne, General S. E. 40
Bryan, William J. 159
Budde, Chuck 245, 246
Buena Vista 89
Byers, William 16
Caldwell, Jonathan 106
Camp Rankin 9
Carlson, Governor 208
Carson, Christopher "Kit" 16, 18
Central City 201
Central Overland California & Pikes Peak Express 3
Cheyenne, Wyoming 180
Chief Colorow 33
Cleveland, President Grover 160
Cody, William "Buffalo Bill" 139, 177, 183
Cody, Wyoming 177
Conger, Dean 241
Cold Springs 5, 7
Colorado Central Railroad 160
Colorado Springs 75, 76, 78, 169
Columbus, Christopher 223
Continental Divide 223
Cornwall, England 69
Cozens, Billy 27, 28, 31
Cozens, Billy 30
Crested Butte 89, 121
Crested Butte 122, 125
Cussler, Clive 52, 53
Cussler, Clive 55
Davidson, George L. O. 105
Del Norte 59
Dellinger, Melvin 264, 265
Dellinger, Melvin 266

DeMandel, Fred 202, 204
Denver Junction 12
Denver Mint 197
Denver Pacific Railroad 39
Denver, South Park & Pacific Railroad 87, 89, 90,
    188
Dolores River 115, 116, 118
Durango 93, 97
Dyer, Father 147
Elijah 241, 242
Elijah 240, 243
Evans, Buelah Beeler 192, 210
Evans, Charles T. 259-263
Evans, Governor John 40
Evanston, Wyoming 177
Fairplay 89, 187, 188, 190, 207, 215, 217
Fairplay 216
Farnham, Mary A. 111, 112
Fincher, Jonathan C. 147
Fort Collins 236, 237
Fort Craig 15
Fort Laramie 15
Fort Sedgwick 10
Fox, E. L. 153, 154
Fulton, Kate 45, 46
Gardner, Charles 15
Georgetown 220
Goddard, Roland 197
Graham, Sue 174
Gray Goose Airways 106
Greeno, Bob 246
Grinnell, Dr. Joseph 194
Gunnison 87, 89, 227, 229, 239

ABOUT THE AUTHOR

Bizarre Colorado is Kenneth Jessen's fifth book. His other books include *Railroads of Northern Colorado*, *Thompson Valley Tales*, *Eccentric Colorado*, and *Colorado Gunsmoke*. Ken also authored three booklets: *Built to Haul Sugar Beets*, *Trolley Cars of Fort Collins*, and *The Wyoming/Colorado Railroad*. In addition, Ken has over 250 articles to his credit in magazines like *Colorado Heritage*, *Rail Classics*, *Trains*, *Old West*, *Frontier Times*, *True West*, and *Colorado Country Life*. He also appeared on several radio and television shows and has given lectures throughout the northern part of the state.

Ken is one of the founders and the past president of The Western Outlaw-Lawman History Association. In addition, Ken has served on the advisory board for the National Association for Outlaw and Lawman History and the Outlaw Trail IIistory Association. Ken is widely published in this field of Western history.

In addition to historical material, Kenneth Jessen has written numerous technical articles covering almost every trade publication in the electronics industry, both in the U.S. and in Europe. He contributed to two McGraw-Hill technical books on electronics.

Ken's education includes a BSEE and MBA from the University of Utah in Salt Lake City. He has worked for Hewlett-Packard as an engineer since 1965, both in California and at their Loveland facility. Ken enjoys traveling, hiking, and skiing in the Rocky Mountain West. Ken and his wife Sonje have three sons, Todd, Chris, and Ben.